READERS THEATRE
FOR YOUNG ADULTS

READERS THEATRE FOR YOUNG ADULTS

Scripts and Script Development

KATHY HOWARD LATROBE
University of Oklahoma

MILDRED KNIGHT LAUGHLIN
University of Oklahoma

TEACHER IDEAS PRESS
A Division of
Libraries Unlimited, Inc.
Englewood, Colorado
1989

TEACHER IDEAS PRESS
A Division of
Libraries Unlimited, Inc.
P.O. Box 6633
Englewood, CO 80155-6633

Library of Congress Cataloging-in-Publication Data

Latrobe, Kathy Howard.
    Readers theatre for young adults : scripts and script development
/ Kathy Howard Latrobe, Mildred Knight Laughlin.
    xi, 130 p.   22x28 cm.
    Bibliography: p. 121.
    Includes index.
    ISBN 0-87287-743-4
    1. Reader's theater--Study and teaching (Secondary) 2. Drama-
-Collections. 3. Fiction--Adaptations. 4. Young adult fiction,
American--Adaptations. 5. Young adult drama, American--Study and
teaching (Secondary) 6. Drama in education. I. Laughlin, Mildred.
II. Title.
PN2081.R4L38   1989
808.5'45--dc20
                                        89-4552
                                        CIP

For our daughters

Barbara and Debra

and

Kimberly and Maria

CONTENTS

PART III—SUGGESTED SCRIPTS

PREFACE

Student enjoyment of literature is a prime concern of all secondary English teachers and school librarians, and readers theatre is one technique to use in developing that pleasure. With that in mind, this book was developed with two major purposes. First, we believe that students will enjoy the experience of doing readers theatre as a part of enjoying a literary piece. Second, we believe that there is great value in having students experiment with the writing of a readers theatre script. Such an activity works well into both writing and whole language experiences. As young people learn the techniques of developing scripts from adolescent books read, they are provided with a pleasurable alternative to the traditional book report. The higher levels of thinking skills required to create and share readers theatre effectively make the process a valuable learning experience.

The book is divided into three parts. Part I provides an overview of the techniques that are recommended and applied by the authors. The importance of readers theatre is emphasized. Directions are given for script selection, scripting techniques, the selection and preparation of readers, and presentation techniques. It is designed to familiarize teachers with the readers theatre process and to guide them in teaching young people to utilize the technique.

Part II provides a treasury of sixteen completed scripts from selected classics recommended in the *Junior High School Library Catalog* and the *Senior High School Library Catalog* (New York: H. W. Wilson). These can be reproduced and used by classes as they are.

Part III contains forty readers theatre starters. Young adult novels that have literary excellence, reader appeal, and potential for a dynamic presentation have been chosen. Each presents a setting, a beginning, and an ending. Students are to write their own scripts for presentation using these starters. The teacher can duplicate these starters as needed for classes or individual students.

We hope that this unique mode of student involvement in literature will increase their comprehension, improve their writing skills, challenge their creativity, build their oral presentation abilities, and finally, increase their enjoyment of literature as they share literature together.

Part I
READERS THEATRE

INTRODUCTION

WHAT READERS THEATRE IS

Readers theatre is a medium involving group reading of a literary script focusing on dialogue between two or more delineated characters who, through voice and bodily tension rather than movement, cause the audience to sense imaginatively characterization, setting, and action. Readers theatre is particularly appropriate to the school setting. Young people sit while reading the lines, thus having the opportunity to concentrate on voice interpretation rather than the practice of action inherent in the presentation of a play. Because of the imaginative participational role of the audience, no character makeup, props, full costumes, scenery, and full-scale stage movement are needed.

Definitions and suggested techniques for presentation often vary, although basic principles remain constant. In this work the emphasis will be on vivid reading rather than any across-stage movement. Any costuming that may be suggested for a character will only be utilized to assist the audience in quickly identifying the reader when there are several in the cast. Those authors who recommend costuming and action on stage negate Leslie Irene Coger and Melvin R. White's concept of "Theatre of the Mind" and reduce the differentiation between readers theatre and drama.[1]

It is also recommended in this work that the readers focus their attention on the audience rather than the person on stage to whom the particular lines are addressed. Skilled interpretation of lines directed offstage allows the imaginative participation needed for the audience to fill in the suggested characterization, action, and setting implied by the readers.

No suggestions will be given for writing original scripts, since the purpose of this work is to encourage young people to participate in readers theatre, inspiring students to read the entire novel from which the excerpt was taken. If young people begin by using a prepared script, they understand the format, techniques, and importance of voice and bodily interpretation of emotions. Then, after that experience and guidance in scripting, young people should be able to adapt a scene from a favorite book for readers theatre.

WHY READERS THEATRE

Participation in readers theatre has many values. Because readers theatre is fun, it makes the literature from which it was adapted a pleasurable experience. Through careful selection of scenes to present, many in the audience should be inspired to read the entire work. In order for young people to prepare a script, they often read a number of books in more than one genre, thus extending their knowledge of quality literature.

Through oral reading the participant develops a greater understanding of the lines. In order to reproduce the text through voice and bodily interpretation of emotions, the reader must experience the author's intention and comprehend fully the meaning of the entire literary work. Personal decisions about theme, plot, characterization, point of view, and setting are basic to structural criticism, and this analysis will deepen the ability of young people to read critically.

Practice in communication skills is inherent in readers theatre. Voice projection, appropriate inflection, and accurate pronunciation are necessary if the work is to be presented in an understandable, moving manner. For the shy young person who fears standing and speaking in front of peers, the participatory experience of reading while seated, a situation where attention is not constantly focused on one person, helps develop confidence and poise. In addition, as young people plan and work together as a cohesive group, they learn to respect the opinions of others and develop skills in the art of cooperation.

Readers theatre inspires creative thinking. Performance demands that the interpreter cause the audience to suspend disbelief, to accept the character, and to sense the mood. Scripting calls for discrimination in selecting an appropriate scene, deciding on transitions best presented by a narrator, adapting or omitting lines if necessary to enhance the presentation, and making the needed introduction to set the scene for the audience. Thus, in addition to critical thinking, scripting gives practice in writing skills.

The audience must engage in concentrated listening in order to gain the most from a presentation. As the text is read, the audience must through imagination create setting, character, and emotion, filling in all aspects merely suggested by the reader. This participation usually means that each listener grasps greater meaning from the excerpt than would be possible from most silent reading. For a generation of young people accustomed to television's dialogue supported by detailed visuals, this stimulus for imaginative listening is invaluable.

WHAT TO USE FOR A SCRIPT

Although fiction traditionally provides the most popular and easily adapted sources for readers theatre scripts, other genres of literature also offer rich possibilities. Biography, folklore, and poetry are often used. For example, Paul Fleischman in *I Am Phoenix* and *Joyful Noise* provides excellent two-part presentations for reading.[2] A series of these poems with narrator introduction and theme tie-in could provide an exciting, thought-provoking presentation.

Although plays are a possible source, in general they are more difficult for the novice script writer to select and adapt. The dependence on action in plays to assist the audience in understanding the lines provides a stumbling block for meaningful adaptation to readers theatre format.

HOW TO SELECT A SCRIPT

Scripts for readers theatre can be adapted from a wide range of materials, but if the purpose is to introduce young people to quality literature, then literary excellence is an important consideration. In addition, the work must have dramatic appeal so the excerpt used will evoke the desired audience reaction and interaction. If the listeners are to enjoy and remember the experience, the selection must be a meaningful, complete segment that gives an insight into the entire work even though it may never be read.

The selection must have emotional appeal, provoking the imagination of the listener and deepening his or her response. This involvement necessitates unique characters, irresistible in their appeal, who strongly interact with each other so audience interest is aroused. The dramatic conflict engaged in by the characters need not demand physical action. The conflict can be within the character, and the action is suggested through narration and conversation. Though some action may be summarized by the narrator, the audience is much more involved when the implied action is part of the dialogue.

It is much easier to create the script if the scene selected has a predominance of conversation and a limited number of characters. Audience interest is lost if the narrator dominates a scene. If too many characters are included, the audience has difficulty identifying each and establishing necessary relationships.

The language employed in the text must be provocative so that audience enjoyment is increased. Through the use of sensory images, thought-provoking references, and figurative language, the listener is able to relate imaginatively to each character.

SCRIPTING TECHNIQUES

Scripting techniques vary according to the nature of the material, the experience of the readers and audience, and time restraints. The following suggestions for preparation of scripts are general in nature and applicable to all scripting efforts.

Anyone preparing a script should read the entire work from which a selection is to be taken. Consideration should be given to the author's purpose in writing, the theme, the mood, the point of view, and which scene or scenes will best give the spirit of the whole. After the portion of the work to be presented is selected, it should be read again to mark those lines that must be kept if the scene is to be understood by an involved audience. If a duplicator is available, pages may be reproduced and a felt-tipped pen used to highlight those speeches.

After another re-reading, unnecessary description or narration should be omitted. If needed, narrator speeches may be developed to bridge gaps, show lapses of time, or summarize action. Authors identify speakers to the reader through *she said* types of devices. In readers theatre it is often necessary to include the name of the character to whom the conversation is directed in order to assist the audience in quick character identification.

Because too many readers on stage are confusing to the audience, it may be appropriate to cut minor characters and give their lines to major characters. This must be done without destroying the spirit of the scene, however. Some authors advise using one reader for two characters. If this must be done, an addition of a hat, glasses, or other slight costume device for one character may be a means by which the audience quickly identifies the speaker. If possible, the need for this approach should be avoided.

As appropriate, a description of the tone of voice—e.g., *angrily*, and a needed gesture or facial expression to assist the reader in presenting each segment may be added. The person preparing the script has a more confident grasp of the whole and a better feeling for the overall emotional impact of the work than any one reader has, even though all presenters should have read the entire book.

The final version of the script should be typed. Double-spacing assists the reader, and bold capital letters giving each character's name should precede the lines of dialogue. Specific directions for tone of voice or gesture should be in parentheses following the name so the reader will not be confused. These directions may also be included within the speech if a change of tone or bodily action is needed. When the script demands the nonverbal communication of emotion by a character who is not reading, that character should be identified as though he or she were speaking, and appropriate directions should be given in parentheses.

Scripts may be prepared on legal-size paper folded to create two columns of type, stapled in the center to resemble a pamphlet, and covered with black paper to appear unobtrusive to the audience. At the beginning of the script the type and location of the seating should be sketched for each character.

Because the setting is imagined by the audience, seating is important. The arrangement of characters on the stage can be a means by which the audience sees character relationships. Seating of the readers may be on the floor, on stools, or on chairs. For some scripts, seating may show importance of characters with the leading character in the center on a stool. If two different groups interact, one early and another late in the scene, the most involved character may be in the center and the grouping on each side shows an event progression. One should experiment with seating until the desired relationship is achieved. Usually a straight line is avoided unless dictated by the script, as would be the case if the setting were the front seat of an automobile. All characters should face the audience so the facial expression of each can be seen. The narrator usually stands at one side, facing the audience and using a lectern for the script.

At the beginning of the scene, the characters should be introduced. In addition to the name, a succinct description of each will aid the audience in remembering who the characters are. Information about preceding events and identification of setting and mood will help the audience understand the scene to be presented. This information is usually given by the narrator. When a first person point of view makes a narrator unnecessary, the person telling the story usually introduces the characters and scene.

If several scenes are presented, a balance should be provided between those that are strongly emotional and ones that are more quiet and relaxed. The narrator usually provides the link between scenes. Characters may change position between scenes as the script dictates.

Although the portion presented is a complete segment, the narrator usually closes with a summary statement tying the scene to the entire work, indicating theme and mood as appropriate, and suggesting the types of events that are to come. Care must be taken not to spoil the desire of the audience to read the book.

HOW TO SELECT/PREPARE READERS

In selecting readers for a classroom or library activity, it is important to remember that the purpose of the activity is to introduce literature and to be a learning experience rather than a polished performance. The reader's enthusiasm for the activity and desire to interpret the script in the best manner possible are important elements.

If the appropriate number have volunteered to participate, it may be well to ask that each reads the entire script before parts are assigned. Sometimes the teacher or librarian may read the script aloud as each young person reads silently. This procedure guides the group in the manner in which the scene may be presented and clears up difficulties in pronunciation of words. However, there is a negative aspect to this approach. Some readers may attempt to imitate the teacher or librarian instead of using individual creativity and imagination.

The better approach may be for the teacher or librarian to introduce the scene followed by the group reading the entire script aloud, taking turns so all have a chance to read. A discussion of each character's personality and the mood to be evoked in the scene should follow. At this time, correct pronunciation for unfamiliar words can be suggested. Students may volunteer for characters they wish to interpret. After the readers highlight their speeches with a pencil or felt-tipped pen and read the lines silently, the whole script may be read again with each participant reading the appropriate segments.

An accurate and meaningful oral interpretation requires that each reader be familiar with the entire work from which the selection is taken. An understanding of each character's personality is essential and should be discussed by the cast. In addition, it may be helpful for the entire group to discuss why the author used certain verbs or adjectives. This may heighten each reader's sensitivity to the script, to the role of each character, and to the emotional involvement desired for the audience.

PRESENTATION TECHNIQUES

If the readers desire to do so, they may wear clothing colors that reflect the mood of the scene. Dark colors may be chosen for serious presentations and lighter colors for humorous presentations. Young people should select clothing that does not distract the audience. Noisy jewelry should be avoided. If desired, an accessory typical of the character to be interpreted may be used, such as a bow tie or a bright scarf. If used, the purpose is to aid the audience in character identification.

Uniformity in size and style of script is needed. A black construction paper cover is often used. Readers should not turn the page at the same time, as this action could be distracting to the audience. Scripts should be so familiar to readers that they can glance at the lines and still maintain eye contact with the audience during reading.

Because the audience is actively, imaginatively involved in the text, the focus of the readers should be on the audience rather than each other. Thus characters do not look directly at each other as they speak the lines, but rather their focuses cross at a point somewhere in the audience. This offstage focus keeps the concentration of everyone on the lines rather than the readers.

Voice projection is a necessary aspect of readers theatre. If the reader is constantly mentally and physically alert to the lines and is concentrating on the scene, it is easier to read with expression and be heard by the audience. Readers must imagine they are experiencing the sensations evident in the lines. The reader as well as the audience must create word pictures. Readers should listen to the speeches of others and be aware of the mood. Even though the scene has been practiced, the presentation should be enthusiastic and have a *first-time nature*.

DETERMINING THE SUCCESS OF THE PRESENTATION

The audience reaction to the presentation is the best evidence of its success. Increased reading by young people of the literary work from which the scene was taken should be another indicator of the value of the presentation. As readers theatre becomes a part of classroom/library activities, improved audience listening skills, increased desire by young people to write their own scripts, and more sensitive portrayal of lines should result. Most of all, readers theatre should be pleasurable just as reading should be pleasurable.

NOTES

[1]Leslie Irene Coger and Melvin R. White, *Readers Theatre Handbook*, rev. ed. (Glenview, Ill.: Scott, Foresman, 1973).

[2]Paul Fleischman, *I Am Phoenix* (New York: Harper & Row, 1985); Fleischman, *Joyful Noise* (New York: Harper & Row, 1988).

Part II
COMPLETED SCRIPTS

This section includes sixteen completed scripts from selected classics. Classics have been emphasized for two reasons. First, with today's increased focus on these works, a variety of techniques are needed to make their study a pleasurable experience. Readers theatre provides one avenue. Second, because many of the classics are familiar to students, they provide an appropriate resource for learning the techniques of readers theatre. This familiarity is important because young people must have read a work before it can be interpreted effectively.

Before young people share the readers theatre scripts, the teacher or librarian should present the concepts outlined in part I. The students will need to understand presentation techniques.

WUTHERING HEIGHTS
Emily Brontë

This script is taken from chapter 9.

STAGING

The narrator stands at a lectern; Catherine and Nelly sit in chairs.

Cathy Earnshaw
X

Nelly Dean
X

Narrator
X

NARRATOR: This particular scene is from *Wuthering Heights* by Emily Brontë. The characters are Catherine Earnshaw, who has grown up wild and undisciplined on the English moors but who is now a proud young lady of twenty-two years, read by _____, and Nelly Dean, a nurse in the Earnshaw home, read by _____. I, _____, am the narrator.

This scene takes place in the kitchen of the Earnshaw home. Unknown to Catherine and Nelly, a third character slumps in the corner. That unseen individual is Heathcliff, a moody and sulky young man who as an orphan had been taken into the Earnshaw household. Catherine has been his friend and his love in this hostile family, dominated by Catherine's jealous and vindictive brother Hindley. Recently Catherine has been courted by Edgar Linton, and she is no longer Heathcliff's loyal and supportive friend. As the scene begins, Catherine has entered the kitchen where Nelly sits rocking Hindley's baby boy.

CATHERINE: Are you alone, Nelly?

NELLY: Yes, Miss.

CATHERINE: (disturbed and anxious) Where's Heathcliff?

NELLY: About his work in the stable.

CATHERINE: Oh, dear! I'm very unhappy!

NELLY:	(somewhat sarcastically because of her unhappiness at Catherine's recent treatment of Heathcliff) A pity. You're hard to please: so many friends and so few cares, and can't make yourself content!
CATHERINE:	Nelly, will you keep a secret for me?
NELLY:	(sulkily) Is it worth keeping?
CATHERINE:	Yes, and it worries me, and I must let it out! I want to know what I should do. Today, Edgar Linton has asked me to marry him, and I've given him an answer. Now, before I tell you whether it was a consent or denial, you tell me which it ought to have been.
NELLY:	Really, Miss Catherine, how can I know? To be sure, considering the exhibition you performed in his presence this afternoon, I might say it would be wise to refuse him: since he asked after that, he must be either hopelessly stupid or a venturesome fool.
CATHERINE:	(peevishly) If you talk so, I won't tell you any more. I accepted him, Nelly. Be quick, and say whether I was wrong!
NELLY:	You accepted him! Then what good is it discussing the matter? You have pledged your word, and cannot retract.
CATHERINE:	(irritated and frowning) But, say whether I should have done so—do!
NELLY:	(moralizing) There are many things to be considered before that question can be answered properly. First and foremost, do you love Mr. Edgar?
CATHERINE:	Who can help it? Of course I do.
NELLY:	Why do you love him, Miss Catherine?
CATHERINE:	Nonsense, I do—that's sufficient.
NELLY:	By no means; you must say why?
CATHERINE:	Well, because he is handsome, and pleasant to be with.
NELLY:	Bad!
CATHERINE:	And because he is young and cheerful.
NELLY:	Bad, still.
CATHERINE:	And because he loves me.
NELLY:	Indifferent, coming there.

CATHERINE: And he will be rich, and I shall like to be the greatest woman of the neighbourhood, and I shall be proud of having such a husband.

NELLY: Worst of all. And now say how you love him?

CATHERINE: As everybody loves — You're silly, Nelly.

NELLY: Not at all — Answer.

CATHERINE: I love the ground under his feet, and the air over his head, and everything he touches, and every word he says. I love all his looks, and all his actions, and him entirely and altogether. There now!

NELLY: And why?

CATHERINE: (frowning) Nay, you are making a jest of it: it is exceedingly ill-natured! It's no jest to me!

NELLY: (seriously) I'm very far from jesting, Miss Catherine. You love Mr. Edgar, because he is handsome, and young, and cheerful, and rich, and loves you. The last, however, goes for nothing: you would love him without that, probably; and with it you wouldn't, unless he possessed the four former attractions.

CATHERINE: No, to be sure not: I should only pity him — hate him, perhaps, if he were ugly, and a clown.

NELLY: But there are several other handsome, rich young men in the world: handsomer, possibly, and richer than he is. What should hinder you from loving them?

CATHERINE: If there be any, they are out of my way: I've seen none like Edgar.

NELLY: You may see some: and he won't always be handsome, and young, and may not always be rich.

CATHERINE: He is now; and I have only to do with the present. I wish you would speak rationally.

NELLY: Well, that settles it; if you have only to do with the present, marry Mr. Linton.

CATHERINE: I don't want your permission for that — I *shall* marry him; and yet you have not told me whether I'm right.

NELLY: Perfectly right: if people be right to marry only for the present. And now, let us hear what you are unhappy about. Your brother will be pleased.... The old lady and gentleman will not object, I think; you will escape from a disorderly, comfortless home into a wealthy, respectable one; and you love Edgar, and Edgar loves you. All seems smooth and easy; where is the obstacle?

CATHERINE: (striking one hand on her forehead and then on her breast) *Here*! and *here*! in whichever place the soul lives. In my soul and in my heart, I'm convinced I'm wrong!

NELLY: That's very strange! I cannot make it out.

CATHERINE: It's my secret. But if you will not mock at me, I'll explain it: I can't do it distinctly; but I'll give you a feeling of how I feel. (sadly) Nelly, do you never dream?

NELLY: Yes, now and then.

CATHERINE: And so do I. I've dreamt in my life dreams that have stayed with me ever after, and changed my ideas; they've gone through and through me, like wine through water, and altered the colour of my mind. And this is one: I'm going to tell it — but take care not to smile at any part of it.

NELLY: Oh! don't, Miss Catherine! We're dismal enough without conjuring up ghosts and visions to perplex us.

CATHERINE: (determined) Nelly, I shall oblige you to listen. It's not long, and I've no power to be merry tonight.

NELLY: (hastily) I won't hear it, I won't hear it!

CATHERINE: If I were in heaven, Nelly, I should be extremely miserable.

NELLY: (with sarcasm) Because you are not fit to go there. All sinners would be miserable in heaven.

CATHERINE: But it is not for that. I dreamt once that I was there.

NELLY: I tell you I won't harken to your dreams, Miss Catherine! I'll go to bed.

CATHERINE: (laughing) This nothing. I was only going to say that heaven did not seem to be my home; and I broke my heart with weeping to come back to earth. The angels were so angry that they flung me out into the middle of the heath on the top of Wuthering Heights; where I woke sobbing for joy. That will do to explain my secret, as well as the other. I've no more business to marry Edgar Linton than I have to be in heaven. If that wicked man, my brother, had not brought Heathcliff so low, I shouldn't have thought of it. It would degrade me to marry Heathcliff now, so he shall never know how I love him. And, I love him not because he's handsome, Nelly, but because he's more myself than I am. Whatever our souls are made of, his and mine are the same; and Linton's is as different as a moonbeam from lightning, or frost from fire. If all else perished, and *Heathcliff* remained, I should still continue to be; and if all else remained, and if Heathcliff were annihilated, the universe would turn to a mighty stranger and I should not seem a part of it. Nelly, I am Heathcliff! He's always, always in my mind — not as a pleasure, any more than I always a pleasure to myself, but as my own being.

NARRATOR: As Catherine proclaims her love for him, Heathcliff slips quietly out the door. Only Nelly sees him. Catherine's decision to wed Edgar Linton may have been based on the present, but with each passing year the future intrudes. Catherine does not escape from the Earnshaw household into the Linton, but rather brings the Linton into the Earnshaw; and the driving force behind the events that unfold is Heathcliff and his consuming desire for revenge.

SCRIPTING NOTES

1. Because of the reader's need to hold a script, all gestures have been limited to the use of one hand at a time. An example of that limitation occurs when Catherine struck her head and her breast to indicate where the soul lives.

2. Names were limited to one form in order to aid the listening audience. Catherine was also known as "Cathy"; and, although Nelly addressed her by both, "Catherine" was more frequently used in this scene. "Nelly" was selected because Catherine did not use her given name — "Ellen."

3. Various nouns and pronouns were replaced by proper names to aid the listeners. For example, "the wicked man" was replaced by "my wicked brother."

4. The longer sentences were shortened, and more familiar styles of punctuation were substituted in several places.

THE INGENIOUS GENTLEMAN DON QUIXOTE DE LA MANCHA

Miguel de Cervantes

This script is taken from chapter 8 when Don Quixote has his adventure with the windmills.

STAGING
The narrator stands at a lectern. Don Quixote and Sancho Panza sit on stools.

Don Quixote
X

Sancho Panza
X

Narrator
X

NARRATOR: We have chosen to share with you a scene from *Don Quixote* by Cervantes. The characters in this scene are Don Quixote, a befuddled gentleman who imagines himself to be a knight-errant, read by _____, and Sancho Panza, who serves Don Quixote, read by _____. I, _____, am the narrator.

This scene presents an early adventure of Don Quixote who in an effort to right every kind of wrong has determined to roam the world over in full armor and on horseback. As he and his squire Sancho Panza ride across a Spanish plain, they come in sight of thirty or forty windmills.

DON QUIXOTE: (with enthusiasm) Fortune is arranging matters for us better than we could have shaped our plans ourselves. Look, friend Sancho Panza, where thirty or more monstrous giants present themselves, all of whom I mean to engage in battle and slay, and with whose spoils we shall begin to make our fortunes. This is righteous warfare, and it is God's good service to sweep so evil a breed from off the face of the earth.

SANCHO PANZA: (bewildered) What giants?

DON QUIXOTE: Those you see there with the long arms, and some have them nearly two leagues long.

SANCHO PANZA: (patiently) Look, your worship, what we see there are not giants but windmills, and what seem to be their arms are the sails that turned by the wind make the millstone go.

DON QUIXOTE: (impatiently) It is easy to see that you are not used to this business of adventures; those are giants; and if you are afraid, away with you out of this and betake yourself to prayer while I engage them in fierce and unequal combat.

SANCHO PANZA: (shouting) Your worship, do not spur the horse to attack. They are windmills and not giants.

DON QUIXOTE: (shouting) Fly not, cowards and vile beings, for it is a single knight that attacks you.

NARRATOR: A slight breeze springs up, and the great sails begin to move.

DON QUIXOTE: (exclaiming) Though you flourish more arms than a mythical beast, you have to reckon with me.

NARRATOR: Don Quixote commends himself with all his heart to his lady Dulcinea and charges at Rocinante's fullest gallop to fall upon the first mill that stands in front of him. As he drives his lance-point into the sail the wind whirls it to pieces, sweeping with it horse and rider. Both roll over the plain. Sancho hurries to Don Quixote and finds him unable to move.

SANCHO PANZA: God bless me! Did I not tell your worship to mind what you were about for they are only windmills? And no one could have made any mistake about it.

DON QUIXOTE: Hush, friend Sancho, the fortunes of war more than any other are liable to frequent fluctuations; and moreover I think, and it is the truth, that same wizard who carried off my study and books, has turned these giants into mills in order to rob me of the glory of vanquishing them, such is the enmity he bears me; but in the end his wicked arts will avail but little against my good sword.

SANCHO PANZA: God order it as he may. Here, let me help you up again on Rocinante.

NARRATOR: Discussing the late adventure, the two follow the road to Puerto Lapice where Don Quixote believes they will find adventures in abundance. For all that, he grieves at the loss of his lance.

DON QUIXOTE: (grieving) I remember having read how another great Spanish knight, having broken his sword in battle, tore from an oak a huge branch, and with it pounded so many Moors that from that day forth he and his descendants have been honored. I mention this because from the first oak I see I mean to cut such another branch, large and stout like that, with which I am determined and resolved to do such deeds that you will consider yourself very fortunate in being found worthy to come and see them and to be an eyewitness of things that will with difficulty be believed.

SANCHO PANZA: Be that as God will. I believe it all as your worship says it; but straighten yourself a little, for you seem all on one side, maybe from the shaking of the fall.

NARRATOR: Together, Don Quixote on Rocinante and Sancho Panza on a donkey, ride forward, and they do find many adventures. All are difficult to believe and in truth poke fun at seventeenth-century customs. In the end Sancho Panza does see truth in Don Quixote's madness.

SCRIPTING NOTES

1. Instructions were written to help the readers deliver the lines with feeling. Some of those instructions were suggested by the text; others were developed from the interpretation of the adapter.

2. Whenever possible lines of description were incorporated into the dialog of the characters; otherwise those lines were assigned to the narrator.

3. "Thee" and "thou" were replaced with contemporary forms.

4. "The giant Briareus" was changed to "a mythical beast."

THE RED BADGE OF COURAGE
Stephen Crane

This script is taken from chapter 1 where Henry and the other soldiers are waiting for the fighting to begin.

STAGING

The narrator stands at a lectern. The three soldiers sit on stools.

                                          Wilson
                                           X

                Henry Fleming
                     X

                                                 Jim Conklin
                                                    X

    Narrator
    X

NARRATOR: The following script is from the first chapter of Stephen Crane's *The Red Badge of Courage*, which is the psychological account of young Henry Fleming's first experiences in combat during the Civil War. In this scene Henry, an uncertain young soldier, read by _____, and two other enlistees, Jim Conklin, the tall soldier, read by _____, and Wilson, the loud soldier, read by _____, face the question of courage under fire. I, _____, am the narrator.

It is a question of courage with which Henry wrestles, and this night he lies on his bunk pondering it. Will he not run from a battle? Previously he had never felt obliged to wrestle too seriously with this question. In his life he had taken certain things for granted, never challenging his belief in ultimate success and bothering little about means and roads. But here he is confronted with a thing of moment. It suddenly appears to him that perhaps in a battle he might run. He is forced to admit that, as far as war is concerned, he knows nothing of himself. Panic and fear grow in his mind and he suddenly sits up.

HENRY:	(with his hand to his forehead) Good Lord, what's th' matter with me? Good Lord!
NARRATOR:	While Henry is deep in his thoughts, the loud soldier and the tall soldier enter the barracks. They are arguing.
THE TALL SOLDIER:	Well, Wilson, yeh kin b'lieve me er not, jest as yeh like. I don't care a hang. Th' army's goin' t' move. All you got to do is to sit down and wait as quiet as you can. Then pretty soon you'll find out I was right.
THE LOUD SOLDIER:	(stubbornly) Well, you don't know everything in the world, do you?
HENRY:	(attempting to appear casual) Going to be a battle, sure, is there, Jim?
THE TALL SOLDIER:	Of course there is. Of course there is. You jest wait 'til tomorrow, and you'll see one of the biggest battles ever was. You jest wait.
HENRY:	(agitated) Oh, thunder!
THE TALL SOLDIER:	(with the air of a man who is about to exhibit a battle for the benefit of his friends) Oh, you'll see fighting this time, my boy, what'll be regular out-and-out fighting.
THE LOUD SOLDIER:	Huh!
HENRY:	Well, like as not this story'll turn out jest like them others did, and we'll stay here, waiting and waiting.
THE TALL SOLDIER:	(exasperated) Not much it won't. Not much it won't. Didn't the cavalry all start this morning? (pausing) The cavalry started this morning. They say there ain't hardly any cavalry left in camp. They're going to Richmond, or some place, while we fight all the Johnnies. It's some dodge like that. The regiment's got orders, too. A feller what seen 'em go to headquarters told me a little while ago. And they're raising blazes all over camp—anybody can see that.
THE LOUD SOLDIER:	(disgusted) Shucks!
HENRY:	(nervously) Jim!
THE TALL SOLDIER:	What?
HENRY:	How do you think the reg'ment 'll do?
THE TALL SOLDIER:	(with cold judgment) Oh, they'll fight all right, I guess, after they once get into it. There's been heaps of fun poked at 'em because they're new, of course, and all that; but they'll fight all right, I guess.

HENRY:	(persisting) Think any of the boys 'll run?
THE TALL SOLDIER:	(tolerantly) Oh, there may be a few of 'em run, but there's them kind in every regiment, 'specially when they first goes under fire. Of course it might happen that the hull kit-and-boodle might start and run, if some big fighting came first-off, and then again they might stay and fight like fun. But you can't bet on nothing. Of course they ain't never been under fire yet, and it ain't likely they'll lick the hull rebel army all-to-once the firs' time; but I think they'll fight better than some, if worse than others. That's the way I figger. They call the reg'ment "fresh fish" and everthing; but the boys come of good stock, and most of 'em 'll fight like sin after they once git shooting. (emphasizing the last four words)
THE LOUD SOLDIER:	(scornfully) Oh, you think you know everything.
HENRY:	Did you ever think you might run yourself, Jim? (laughing as if to mean a joke)
THE LOUD SOLDIER:	(giggles nervously)
THE TALL SOLDIER:	(profoundly) Well, I've thought it might get too hot for Jim Conklin in some of them scrimmages, and if a whole lot of boys started and run, why, I s'pose I'd start and run. And if I once started to run, I'd run like the devil, and no mistake. But if everybody was a-standing and a-fighting, why I'd stand and fight. Be jiminey, I would. I'll bet on it.
THE LOUD SOLDIER:	(scornfully) Huh!
NARRATOR:	The reassurance that the tall soldier gave Henry is short-lived. The army does not move out, and the waiting, the worrying, the self-doubts mount. Finally Henry concludes that the only way to prove himself is to go into the battle and then figuratively to watch his legs to discover their merits and faults. To gain the answer, he needs blaze, blood, and danger. Finally, the opportunity to prove himself comes — not once, but again and again; and Henry learns not only about his cowardice and fear but also about his courage and endurance.

SCRIPTING NOTES

1. The narrator's lines are in the present tense, not the past tense of the novel.

2. Some of the colloquial expressions have been adapted to other forms, for example, "oncet" has been changed to "once."

3. The characters' movements described in the text have been either omitted (e.g., Henry's springing from the bunk and his pacing) or included in the narrator's lines (e.g., the account of the tall soldier and the loud soldier's entrance).

4. Words or phrases that would be obscure to a listening audience were either omitted (e.g., "rapid altercation, in which they fastened upon each other various strange epithets") or changed (e.g., "arguing" in place of "wrangling").

5. An informed presentation requires that the script contain numerous directions for the readers. Most of those directions were taken from the original text although some were created by the adapter.

6. The narrator's reference to the Civil War was not taken from the original text, but rather from assumptions of various critics.

THE PERSONAL HISTORY OF DAVID COPPERFIELD

Charles Dickens

This script is taken from chapter 8, "My Holidays: Especially One Happy Afternoon."

STAGING

The narrator stands at a lectern; David stands; other characters sit in chairs.

Mr. Murdstone
X

Clara Murdstone
X

David
X

Jane Murdstone
X

Narrator
X

NARRATOR:	The script that we have chosen to share is from *The Personal History of David Copperfield* by Charles Dickens. The characters in this scene are David Copperfield at age ten, read by _____; his timid mother Clara Murdstone, read by _____; his cruel stepfather Mr. Murdstone, read by _____; and his stepfather's critical sister Jane Murdstone, read by _____. I, _____, am the narrator.
	David Copperfield has returned home on a holiday from boarding school in London; however, the home of his younger years changed forever when the overbearing and cruel Mr. Murdstone married David's mother and with his equally unpleasant sister moved into David's home. David's resolution has been to keep himself as much out of their way as possible, but even that approach fails him.
MR. MURDSTONE:	(coldly) David, I am sorry to observe that you are of a sullen disposition.
DAVID:	(stands still, head down)

JANE MURDSTONE:	(hatefully) As sulky as a bear!
MR. MURDSTONE:	Now David, a sullen obdurate disposition is, of all tempers, the worst.
JANE MURDSTONE:	And the boy's is, of all such dispositions that ever I have seen, the most confirmed and stubborn. I think, my dear Clara, even you must observe it?
CLARA MURDSTONE:	(hesitantly) I beg your pardon, my dear Jane, but are you quite sure — I am certain you'll excuse me, my dear Jane — that you understand Davy?
JANE MURDSTONE:	I should be somewhat ashamed of myself, Clara, if I could not understand the boy, or any boy. I don't profess to be profound; but I do lay claim to common sense.
CLARA MURDSTONE:	No doubt, my dear Jane, your understanding is very vigorous —
JANE MURDSTONE:	(angrily) Oh dear, no! Pray don't say that, Clara.
CLARA MURDSTONE:	But I am sure it is, and everybody knows it is. I profit so much by it myself in many ways — at least I ought to — that no one can be more convinced of it than myself; and therefore I speak with great diffidence, my dear Jane, I assure you.
JANE MURDSTONE:	We'll say I don't understand the boy, Clara. We'll agree, if you please, that I don't understand him at all. He is much too deep for me. But perhaps my brother's penetration may enable him to have some insight into his character. And I believe my brother was speaking on the subject when we — not very decently — interrupted him.
MR. MURDSTONE:	(in a low grave voice) I think, Clara, that there may be better and more dispassionate judges of such a question than you.
CLARA MURDSTONE:	(timidly) Edward, you are a far better judge of all questions than I pretend to be. Both you and Jane are. I only said —
MR. MURDSTONE:	(interrupting) You only said something weak and inconsiderate. Try not to do it again, my dear Clara, and keep a watch upon yourself.
CLARA MURDSTONE:	(whispering) Yes, my dear Edward.
MR. MURDSTONE:	I was sorry, David, I remarked to observe that you are of a sullen disposition. This is not a character that I can suffer to develop itself beneath my eyes without an effort at improvement. You must endeavour, sir, to change it. We must endeavour to change it for you.

DAVID:	I beg your pardon, sir. I have never meant to be sullen since I came back.
MR. MURDSTONE:	(fiercely) Don't take refuge in a lie, sir! You have withdrawn yourself in your sullenness to your own room. You have kept to your own room when you ought to have been here. You know now, once for all, that I require you to be here, and not there. Further, that I require you to bring obedience here. You know me, David, I will have it done.
JANE MURDSTONE:	(chuckles hoarsely)
MR. MURDSTONE:	I will have a respectful, prompt, and ready bearing towards myself and towards Jane Murdstone, and towards your mother. I will not have this room shunned as if it were infected, at the pleasure of a child. (commanding David as he would command a dog) Sit down.
DAVID:	(sits in a nearby chair)
MR. MURDSTONE:	One thing more, I observe that you have an attachment to low and common company. You are *not* to associate with servants. The kitchen will not improve you in the many respects in which you need improvement. Of the woman who abets you, I say nothing—since you, Clara, from old associations and long-established fancies, have a weakness respecting her which is not yet overcome.
JANE MURDSTONE:	A most unaccountable delusion it is!
MR. MURDSTONE:	I only say that I disapprove of your preferring such company as the maid Mistress Peggotty, and that it is to be abandoned. Now, David, you understand me, and you know what will be the consequence if you fail to obey me to the letter.
NARRATOR:	David's history began with his wondering whether he will "... turn out to be the hero of his own life, or whether that station will be held by anybody else...." Who that hero will be depends in part on how he resolves his childhood conflict with Mr. Murdstone. The challenge is David's and David's alone, and the challenge will become more difficult.

SCRIPTING NOTES

1. This script, flowing from the dialog of the novel, required no changes in the lines.

2. The adaptation added only instructions for communicating mood and emotion through body language and voice.

A TALE OF TWO CITIES

Charles Dickens

This script is taken from chapter 4, "The Preparation."

STAGING

The narrator stands at a lectern; the other characters sit in chairs.

Mr. Jarvis Lorry   Miss Lucie Manette

X   X

Narrator

X

NARRATOR: This scene is from Charles Dickens's novel *A Tale of Two Cities*. The characters are Mr. Jarvis Lorry, a reserved banker from London, read by _____; Miss Lucie Manette, a pretty seventeen-year-old, read by _____. I, _____, am the narrator.

This scene is set at an inn in Dover; the year is 1775. Mr. Lorry and Miss Manette have met so that Mr. Lorry may disclose a remarkable discovery: that her father, long believed to be dead, is alive in Paris. Because he is afraid of Miss Manette's over-reaction, he talks around the message, hesitating frequently and apologizing for a businesslike approach.

MISS MANETTE: I received a letter from the Bank, sir, yesterday, informing that some intelligence — or discovery —

MR. LORRY: (interrupting) The word is not material, miss; either word will do.

MISS MANETTE: — respecting the small property of poor father, whom I never — so long dead — render it necessary that I should go to Paris, there to communicate with a gentleman of the Bank, so good as to be despatched to Paris for the purpose.

MR. LORRY: Myself.

MISS MANETTE: As I was prepared to hear, sir. I replied to the Bank, sir, that as it considered necessary, by those who know, and who are so kind as to advise me, that I should go to France, and that as I am an orphan and have no friend who could go with me, I should esteem it highly if I might be permitted to place myself, during the journey, under your protection. After you had left London, I think a messenger was sent to beg the favour of your waiting for me here.

MR. LORRY: I was happy to be entrusted with the charge. I shall be more happy to execute it.

MISS MANETTE: Sir, I thank you indeed. I thank you very gratefully. It was told me by the Bank that you would explain to me the details of the business, and that I must prepare myself to find them of a surprising nature. I have done my best to prepare myself, and I naturally have a strong and eager interest to know what they are.

MR. LORRY: Naturally. Yes—I—(slight pause)—It is very difficult to begin.

MISS MANETTE: Are you quite a stranger to me, sir?

MR. LORRY: Am I not? (Opens hand and extends it outward with an argumentative smile.) In your adopted country, I presume, I cannot do better than address you as a young English lady, Miss Manette?

MISS MANETTE: If you please, sir.

MR. LORRY: Miss Manette, I am a man of business. I have a business charge to acquit myself of. In your reception of it, don't heed me any more than if I was a speaking machine—truly, I am not much else. I will, with your leave, relate to you, miss, the story of one of our customers.

MISS MANETTE: (surprised) Story!

MR. LORRY: (in a hurry) Yes, customers; in the banking business we usually call our connection our customers. He is a French gentleman; a scientific gentleman; a man of great acquirements—a doctor.

MISS MANETTE: Not of Beauvais, my family's home.

MR. LORRY: Why, yes, of Beauvais. Like Monsieur Manette, your father, the gentleman was of Beauvais. Like Monsieur Manette, your father, the gentleman was of repute in Paris. I had the honour of knowing him there. Our relations were business relations, but confidential. I was at that time in our French House, and had been—oh! twenty years.

MISS MANETTE: At that time—I may ask, at what time, sir?

MR. LORRY: I speak, miss, of twenty years ago. He married—an English lady—and I was one of the trustees. His affairs, like the affairs of many other French gentlemen and French families, were entirely in the hands of Tellson Bank. In a similar way I am, or I have been trustee of one kind or other for scores of our customers. These are mere business relations, miss; there is no friendship in them, no particular interest, nothing like sentiment. I have passed from one to another, in the course of my business life, just as I pass from one of our customers to another in the course of my business day; in short, I have no feelings; I am a mere machine. To go on—

MISS MANETTE: But this is my father's story, sir; and I begin to think (frowning) that when I was left an orphan through my mother's surviving my father only two years, it was you who brought me to England. I am almost sure it was you.

MR. LORRY: Miss Manette, it *was* I. And you will see how truly I spoke of myself just now, in saying I had no feelings, and that all the relations I hold with my fellow creatures are mere business relations, when you reflect that I have never seen you since. No; you have been the ward of Tellson's Bank since, and I have been busy with the other business of Tellson's Bank since. Feelings! I have no time for them, no chance of them. I pass my whole life, miss, in turning an immense pecuniary mangle. So far, miss, as you have remarked, this is the story of your regretted father. Now comes the difference. If your father had not died when he did—Don't be frightened!

MISS MANETTE: (jerking with nervousness)

MR. LORRY: How you start! (in a soothing tone) Pray, pray, control your agitation—a matter of business. As I was saying—as I was saying, if Monsieur Manette had not died; if he had suddenly and silently disappeared; if he had been spirited away; if it had not been difficult to guess to what dreadful place, though no art could trace him; if he had an enemy in some compatriot who could exercise a privilege that I in my own time have known the boldest people afraid to speak of in a whisper, across the water there; for instance, the privilege of filling up blank forms for the consignment of any one to the oblivion of a prison for any length of time; if his wife had implored the king, the queen, the court, the clergy for any tidings of him, and all quite in vain—then the history of your father would have been the history of this unfortunate gentleman, the doctor of Beauvais.

MISS MANETTE: I entreat you to tell me more, sir.

MR. LORRY: I will. I am going to. You can bear it?

MISS MANETTE: I can bear anything but the uncertainty you leave me in at this moment.

MR. LORRY: You speak collectedly, and you—*are* collected. That's good! A matter of business. Regard it as a matter of business—business that must be done. Now if this doctor's wife, though a lady of great courage and spirit, had suffered so intensely from this cause before her little child was born—

MISS MANETTE: The little child was a daughter, sir?

MR. LORRY: A daughter. A—a—matter of business—don't be distressed. Miss, if the poor lady had suffered so intensely before her little child was born, that she came to the determination of sparing the poor child the inheritance of any part of the agony she had known the pains of, by rearing her in the belief that her father was dead—

MISS MANETTE: For the truth. O dear, good, compassionate sir, for the truth!

MR. LORRY: That's right, that's right. Courage! Business! You have business before you; useful business. Miss Manette, your mother took this course with you. And when she died—I believe broken-hearted—having never slackened her unavailing search for your father, she left you, at two years old, to grow to be blooming, beautiful, and happy, without the dark cloud upon you of living in uncertainty whether your father soon wore his heart out in prison, or wasted there through many lingering years.

You know that your parents had no great possession, and that what they had was secured to your mother and to you. There has been no new discovery, of money, or of any other property; but—but he has been—been found. He is alive. Greatly changed, it is too probable; almost a wreck, it is possible; though we will hope the best. Still, alive. Your father has been taken to the house of an old servant in Paris, and we are going there: I, to identify him if I can; you, to restore him to life, love, duty, rest, comfort.

MISS MANETTE: (stunned and nearly fainting) I am going to see his ghost! It will be his ghost—not him!

MR. LORRY: There, there, there! See now, see now! The best and the worst are known to you, now. You are well on your way to the poor wronged gentleman, and with a fair sea voyage and a fair land journey, you will be soon at his dear side.

NARRATOR: And, thus begins a tale of two cities — London and Paris, and it is not merely business for even staid Mr. Lorry. It is a tale of war, of assumed names, of secrets long kept, of betrayal, and of sacrifice. It is the account of individuals caught in the turmoil of the French Revolution; and, as Dickens wrote, "It was the best of times, it was the worst of times, ... it was the season of Light, it was the season of Darkness, ... we had everything before us, we had nothing before us...."

SCRIPTING NOTES

1. Movement and description are omitted.

2. Some sentences were shortened for both the readers and the listeners.

3. Instructions for the readers are necessary, especially since the characters in this scene talk around the issues.

4. Contemporary punctuation has been used in place of some of the older forms.

SILAS MARNER

George Eliot

This script is taken from chapter 3 when Godfrey and Dunsey are deciding how to repay their father.

STAGING

The narrator stands at a lectern; Godfrey and Dunsey sit on tall stools.

Godfrey   Dunsey
X   X

Narrator
X

NARRATOR: The script that we have chosen to share is from *Silas Marner* by George Eliot. The characters are two sons of Squire Cass: Godfrey, read by _____, and Dunsey, read by _____. I, _____, am the narrator.

Godfrey and Dunsey fall into an unlikely alliance when Godfrey, blackmailed by Dunsey because of a secret marriage to the lowly Molly Farren, collects rent from one of the Squire's tenants and passes it along to Dunsey. When the Squire, unaware that Godfrey has intercepted the money, determines to press the issue of the missing payment with the tenant, Godfrey calls Dunsey in and demands the money.

DUNSEY: (in a mocking tone) Well, Master Godfrey, what do you want with me? You're my elders and betters, you know; I was obliged to come when you sent for me.

GODFREY: (savagely) This is what I want — and just shake yourself sober and listen, will you? I want to tell you that I must hand over the rent of Fowler's to the Squire, or else tell him I gave it to you; for he's threatening to press for it, and it'll all be out soon, whether I tell him or not. He said, just now, before he went out, he should send word to Cox to collect, if Fowler didn't come and pay up his arrears this week. The Squire's short o' cash, and in no humour to stand any nonsense; and you know what he threatened, if ever he found you making away with his money again. So, see and get the money, and pretty quickly, will you?

DUNSEY: (sneeringly) Oh! Suppose, now, you get the money yourself, and save me the trouble, eh? Since you was so kind as to hand it over to me, you'll not refuse me the kindness to pay it back for me: it was your brotherly love made you do it, you know.

GODFREY: (fiercely) Don't come near me with that look, else I'll knock you down.

DUNSEY: (with vicious sarcasm) Oh no, you won't because I'm such a good-natured brother, you know. I might get turned out of house and home, and cut off with a shilling any day. I might tell the Squire how you, his handsome son, were secretly married to that nice young woman, Molly Farren, and were very unhappy because you couldn't live with your drunken wife, and I should slip into your place as comfortable as could be. But, you see, I don't do it—I'm so easy and good-natured. You'll take any trouble for me. You'll get the hundred pounds for me—I know you will.

GODFREY: (quivering with anger) How can I get the money? I haven't a shilling to bless myself with. And it's a lie that you'd slip into my place: you'd get yourself turned out too, that's all. For if you begin telling tales, I'll follow. Our other brother is my father's favourite—you know that very well. He'd only think himself well rid of you.

DUNSEY: Never mind. It 'ud be very pleasant to me to go in your company—you're such a handsome brother, and we've always been so fond of quarreling with one another, I shouldn't know what to do without you. But you'd like better for us both to stay at home together; I know you would. So you'll manage to get that little sum o' money, and I'll bid you good-bye, though I'm sorry to part.

GODFREY: (shouting) I tell you, I have no money: I can get no money.

DUNSEY: Borrow of old Kimble.

GODFREY: I tell you, he won't lend me any more, and I shan't ask him.

DUNSEY: Well then, sell your horse Wildfire.

GODFREY: Yes, that's easy talking. I must have the money directly.

DUNSEY: Well, you've only got to ride him to the hunt tomorrow. There'll be Bryce and Keating there, for sure. You'll get more bids than one.

GODFREY: (sarcastically) I daresay, and get back home at eight o'clock, splashed up to the chin. I'm going to Mrs. Osgood's birthday dance.

DUNSEY: (turning his head on one side, and speaking in a small mincing treble) Oho! And there's sweet Miss Nancy coming; and we shall dance with her, and promise never to be naughty again, and be taken into favour, and—

GODFREY: (angrily) Hold your tongue about Miss Nancy, you fool, else I'll throttle you.

DUNSEY: (sarcastically) What for? You've a very good chance. I'd advise you to creep up her sleeve again: it 'ud be saving time if Molly should happen to take a drop too much opium someday, and make a widower of you. Miss Nancy wouldn't mind being a second, if she didn't know it. And you've got a good-natured brother, who'll keep your secret well, because you'll be so very obliging to him.

GODFREY: (quivering again with anger) I tell you what it is. My patience is pretty near at an end. If you'd a little more sharpness in you, you might know that you may urge a man a bit too far, and make one leap as easy as another. I don't know but what it is so now: I may as well tell the Squire everything myself—I should get you off my back, if I got nothing else. And, after all, he'll know sometime. Molly's been threatening to come herself and tell him. So, don't flatter yourself that your secrecy's worth any price you choose to ask. You drain me of money till I've got nothing to pacify *her* with, and she'll do as she threatens some day. It's all one. I'll tell my father everything myself, and you may go to the devil.

DUNSEY: (with an air of unconcern) As you please.

GODFREY: (bitterly) It's just like you to talk about my selling Wildfire in that cool way—the last thing I've got to call my own, and the best bit of horseflesh I ever had in my life. And if you'd got a spark of pride in you, you'd be ashamed to see the stables emptied, and everybody sneering about it. But it's my belief you'd sell yourself, if it was only for the pleasure of making somebody feel he'd got a bad bargain.

DUNSEY: (very placably) Ay, ay, you do me justice, I see. You know I'm a jewel for 'ticing people into bargains. For which reason I advise you to let *me* sell Wildfire. I'd ride him to the hunt tomorrow for you, with pleasure. I shouldn't look so handsome as you in the saddle, but it's the horse they'll bid for, and not the rider.

GODFREY: (shouting) Yes, I daresay—trust my horse to you.

DUNSEY: As you please. It's *you* have got to pay Fowler's money; it's none of my business. You received the money from him when you went to Bramcote, and *you* told the Squire it wasn't paid. I'd nothing to do with that; you chose to be so obliging as give it me, that was all. If you don't want to pay the money, let it alone; it's all one to me. But I was willing to accommodate you by undertaking to sell the horse, seeing it's not convenient to you to go so far tomorrow.

GODFREY: (in a half-conciliatory tone) Well, you mean no nonsense about the horse, eh? You'll sell him all fair, and hand over the money? If you don't, you know everything'll go to smash, for I've got nothing else to trust to. And you'll have less pleasure in pulling the house over my head, when your own skull's to be broken too.

DUNSEY: Ay, ay, all right. I thought you'd come round. I'm the fellow to bring old Bryce up to the scratch. I'll get a hundred and twenty for him, if I get you a penny.

GODFREY: But it'll perhaps rain cats and dogs tomorrow, as it did yesterday, and then you can't go.

DUNSEY: Not *it*. I'm always lucky in my weather. It might rain if you wanted to go yourself. You never hold trumps, you know—I always do. You've got the beauty, you see, and I've got the luck, so you must keep me by you for your crooked sixpence; you'll *never* get along without me.

NARRATOR: However, luck fails, and it fails not only for Dunsey, but also for an old miser, Silas Marner. The next day Dunsey kills Wildfire on a high jump, and then he happens upon Silas Marner's stone cottage from which he steals Silas's hoarded income from fifteen years of weaving. Silas is devastated, but his gold is not the last treasure to change hands because of Godfrey Cass's lack of conviction. A second treasure goes *to* Silas, and therein is the story of Silas Marner.

SCRIPTING NOTES

1. Directions for reading the lines flow naturally from the author's text.

2. Several words that may be unfamiliar to today's young adults have been replaced with those that are more contemporary (e.g., opium was substituted for laudanum).

3. The explanation that Wildfire is a horse was incorporated into the dialog.

4. Movement and extraneous conversation (e.g., Dunsey's comment that he wants ale as well as his ringing for it) were omitted.

5. Passages of description (e.g., those describing Godfrey's moral dilemma) were not included in the script; however, they did contribute to the readers' instructions.

6. Dunsey (not the more formal Dunstan which is occasionally found in the text) is used consistently in the script.

7. The last few lines of the scene are omitted in order to use Dunsey's comment on luck as a transition for the narrator's closing lines.

THE HOUSE OF THE SEVEN GABLES
Nathaniel Hawthorne

This script is taken from chapter 7, "The Guest."

STAGING

Narrator stands at a lectern; all other characters sit in chairs.

Hepzibah
X

Clifford   Phoebe
X   X

Narrator
X

NARRATOR: The following script is taken from chapter 7, "The Guest," in Nathaniel Hawthorne's novel *The House of the Seven Gables*. The characters in this scene are worried old Hepzibah Pyncheon, read by _____; her befuddled brother Clifford, read by _____; and Phoebe, a gentle young distant cousin, read by _____. I, _____, am the narrator.

The setting for this scene is the Pyncheon house—the house of the seven gables, built by Colonel Pyncheon in colonial Salem. Colonel Pyncheon had unjustly taken the homesite from Matthew Maul who was subsequently executed as a wizard. At the time of his death, Matthew Maul prophesied that God would give the Pyncheons blood to drink. Colonel Pyncheon's sudden death appeared to fulfill the curse as, years later, did Jaffrey Pyncheon's death. However, Jaffrey Pyncheon's death resulted in a murder trial, and Clifford Pyncheon was unjustly convicted and sentenced to thirty years in the state prison. In the meantime, his sister Hepzibah, a frightened and poverty-stricken recluse, has attempted to support the household by opening a small shop which, through Phoebe's efforts, has been profitable. In this scene, the elderly brother and sister are reunited as Clifford has completed his prison sentence and returned to the house of the seven gables.

HEPZIBAH: (in the tone one uses to soothe a fretful child) Dear Clifford, this is our cousin Phoebe—little Phoebe Pyncheon—cousin Arthur's only child, you know. She has come from the country to stay with us awhile; for our old house has grown to be very lonely now.

CLIFFORD: (somewhat bewildered and with sluggish speech) Phoebe? Phoebe Pyncheon? Phoebe. Arthur's child! Ah, I forget! No matter! She is very welcome.

HEPZIBAH: Come, dear Clifford, take this chair. Please, Phoebe, lower the curtain a little more. Now let us begin breakfast.

CLIFFORD: (murmuring quietly and sadly) Is this you, Hepzibah? How changed! How changed! And are you angry with me? Why do you bend your brow so?

HEPZIBAH: (warmly) Angry! Angry with you, Clifford! There is nothing but love, here, Clifford, nothing but love! You are at home!

CLIFFORD: (smiles feebly, pauses, then with nervous haste) More, more coffee! This is what I need! Give me more. (straightens up in chair, looks more alert)

HEPZIBAH: Of course, Clifford.

CLIFFORD: How pleasant and delightful is that open window. How beautiful that play of sunshine! Those flowers, how very fragrant! Young Phoebe's face, how cheerful! Ah! this must be all a dream! A dream! A dream that hides the four stone walls of prison! (frowning and slumping in his chair, his mood darkens)

PHOEBE: (in a kind, but obvious attempt to cheer him) Here is a new kind of rose, which I found this morning. There will be but five or six on the bush this season. This is the most perfect of them all; not a speck of blight or mildew in it. And how sweet it is! Sweet like no other rose! One can never forget that scent!

CLIFFORD: (eagerly) Ah! Let me see! Let me hold it! Thank you! This has done me good. I remember how I used to prize this flower, long ago, I suppose, very long ago! Or was it only yesterday? It makes me feel young again! Am I young? Either this remembrance is singularly distinct, or this consciousness strangely dim! Thank you. (he lets his eyes drift across the room to a far wall, then he exclaims with force) Hepzibah! Hepzibah! Why do you keep that horrible portrait of Colonel Pyncheon on the wall? I have told you a thousand times that it was the evil curse of the house! My curse particularly. Take it down, at once!

HEPZIBAH: (sadly) Dear Clifford, you know it cannot be!

CLIFFORD: Then, at all events, cover it with a crimson curtain, broad enough to hang in folds, and with a golden border and tassels. I cannot bear it! It must not stare me in the face!

HEPZIBAH: (soothingly) Yes, dear Clifford, the picture shall be covered. There is a crimson curtain in a trunk above stairs, a little faded and moth-eaten I'm afraid, but Phoebe and I will do wonders with it.

CLIFFORD: This very day, remember! Why should we live in this dismal house at all? Why not go to the south of France? To Italy? Paris, Naples, Venice, Rome? Hepzibah will say we have not the means. A clever idea that! (he smiles to himself, then glances sarcastically at Hepzibah)

NARRATOR: Silence falls over the group, and Clifford nearly dozes off to sleep. Suddenly the sharp and peevish tinkle of the shop-bell rings through the house and jars Clifford.

CLIFFORD: Good heavens, Hepzibah! What horrible disturbance have we now in the house? I have never heard such a hateful clamor! Why do you permit it? In the name of all noise, what can it be?

HEPZIBAH: (patient, but embarrassed) Dear Clifford, I wish I could keep the sound from your ears. It is very disagreeable even to me. But, do you know, Clifford, I have something to tell you? Please run, Phoebe, and see who is there! This naughty little tinkle is nothing but our shop-bell.

CLIFFORD: (bewildered) Shop-bell!

HEPZIBAH: (with dignity) Yes, our shop-bell. For you must know, dearest Clifford, that we are very poor. And there was no other resource, but either to accept assistance from a hand that I would push aside, and so would you, were it to offer bread when we were dying for it, no help, save from him, or else to earn our subsistence with my own hands! Alone, I might have been content to starve. But you were to be given back to me! Do you think then, dear Clifford, that I have brought an irretrievable disgrace on the old house, by opening a little shop in the front gable? Our great-great-grandfather did the same, when there was far less need! Are you ashamed of me?

CLIFFORD: (sadly) Shame! Disgrace! Do you speak these words to me, Hepzibah? It was not kind to say so, Hepzibah! After thirty years in prison what shame can befall me now? Are we so very poor, Hepzibah? (looks down as if in deep thought)

HEPZIBAH: (gazes with pity at Clifford)

NARRATOR: Shame, poverty, and isolation have been the curse that the ghost of Matthew Maul has supposedly brought to Clifford and Hepzibah Pyncheon. Furthermore, they are soon to see one more Pyncheon life claimed, and that death will occur hauntingly under the threatening portrait of old Colonel Pyncheon, in the same room and in the same way as the other Pyncheon deaths. Yet, Clifford and Hepzibah are fortunate among all the generations of Pyncheons in the house of seven gables; in a mysterious way Matthew Maul's curse changes to a blessing for them and the succeeding generations of the Pyncheon and Maul families.

SCRIPTING NOTES

1. Certain details were added to several lines so that they would be more intelligible to the audience. For example, "that odious picture" in Clifford's dialogue was changed to "that horrible portrait of Colonel Pyncheon on the wall." Likewise, Clifford's allusion to "stone walls" was changed to "the stone walls of prison."

2. Some of the longer, descriptive elements of the dialogue were omitted.

3. Instances when Clifford absently addressed Hepzibah and Phoebe in the third person were adapted to the second person.

4. The text preceding Clifford's last line was omitted because the rapid mood changes would baffle a readers theatre audience. In that section, Clifford suddenly bursts into brief but emotional tears.

THE SCARLET LETTER
Nathaniel Hawthorne

This script is taken from chapter 8, "The Elf and the Minister."

STAGING

The narrator stands at a lectern; all other characters sit on stools.

Roger Chillingworth   John Wilson
X   X

Pearl   Governor Bellingham
X   X

Hester Prynne   Arthur Dimmesdale
X   X

Narrator
X

NARRATOR: The script which we are reading is adapted from *The Scarlet Letter* by Nathaniel Hawthorne. The characters are a young adulteress, Hester Prynne, read by _____; her three-year-old child, Pearl, read by _____; the powerful Governor Bellingham, read by _____; an old clergyman, John Wilson, read by _____; a young clergyman, Arthur Dimmesdale, read by _____; and an elderly and mysterious physician, Roger Chillingworth, read by _____. I, _____, am the narrator.

Three years ago Hester had been found guilty of adultery, and for her punishment she wears an embroidered A on her bodice. The name of Pearl's father has remained unknown to the villagers, as well as to Hester's secret and estranged husband, Roger Chillingworth. On this particular day, Hester has arrived at the home of Governor Bellingham to deliver a pair of gloves which she has embroidered. However, another and far more compelling reason for her going to seek an interview with the Governor concerns the future of her child. There has been a rumor that the strict church members, especially Governor Bellingham, plan to take Pearl away from her.

This scene takes place in the Governor's garden in colonial Boston. As usual Hester is wearing the elaborately embroidered scarlet A, and Pearl, symbolizing Hester's guilt and joy, is wearing an equally elaborate red dress. As Hester hears the Governor approaching, Pearl begins to cry for one of the garden's red roses.

HESTER: Hush, child, hush! Do not cry, dear little Pearl! I hear voices in the garden. The Governor is coming and gentlemen along with him.

GOVERNOR BELLINGHAM: What have we here? A scarlet clad child of which I have never seen the like, since my days of vanity, in old King James's time, when I was wont to esteem it a high favor to be admitted to a court mask! There used to be a swarm of these small apparitions, in holiday time; and we called them children of the Lord of Misrule. But how got such a guest into my hall?

JOHN WILSON: Ay, indeed. What little bird of scarlet plumage may this be? Pray, young one, who are you, and what has ailed your mother to dress you in this strange fashion? Are you a Christian, child—ha? Do you know your catechism? Or are you one of those naughty elfs whom we thought to have left behind us in merry old England?

PEARL: I am mother's child and my name is Pearl.

JOHN WILSON: Pearl? Ruby, rather! Or Coral! Or Red Rose, at the very least, judging from your hue! But where is this mother of yours? Ah! I see. (in a stage whisper) Governor, this is the selfsame child whom we have been discussing, and there is the unhappy woman, Hester Prynne, her mother!

GOVERNOR BELLINGHAM: Hester Prynne, lately there has been much question concerning you. The point has been weightily discussed whether we, that are of authority and influence, do well discharge our consciences by trusting an immortal soul, such as there is in your child, to the guidance of one who has stumbled and fallen amid the pitfalls of this world. What do you, the mother of this child, have to say? Don't you think your little one could better be disciplined strictly, clad more soberly, and instructed in the truths of heaven and earth if she be taken from your charge? What can you do for the child?

HESTER: (pointing to her heart) I can teach my little Pearl what I have learned from this!

GOVERNOR BELLINGHAM: Woman, that scarlet letter to which you refer is your badge of shame!

HESTER: Nevertheless, this badge has taught me—it daily teaches me—it is teaching me at this moment—lessons by which my child may be wiser and better, although these lessons can profit nothing to me.

GOVERNOR BELLINGHAM: We will judge cautiously. Good Master Wilson, I pray you, question this Pearl and see whether she has had such good Christian nurture as befits a child of her age.

JOHN WILSON: (solemnly) Pearl, you must take heed to instruction, that so, in due season, you may wear in your bosom the pearl of great price. Can you tell me, my child, who made you?

PEARL: (shaking her head to indicate "no")

NARRATOR: Now Pearl knows well enough who made her, for Hester Prynne, the daughter of a pious home, had taught her about her Heavenly Father. But that perversity, which all children have more or less, takes possession of her. Then she answers.

PEARL: I have not been made at all. My mother plucked me off the bush of wild roses that grows by the prison door!

GOVERNOR BELLINGHAM: (slowly recovering from his astonishment) This is awful! Here is a child of three years old, and she cannot tell who made her! Without question, she is equally in the dark as to her soul, its present depravity, and future destiny! Gentlemen, we need inquire no further.

HESTER: (with great emotion) God gave me the child. He gave her in requital of all things else which he had taken from me. She is my happiness! She is my torture, none the less! Pearl keeps me here in life! Pearl punishes me too! Don't you see, she is the scarlet letter, only capable of being loved, and so endowed with a millionfold the power of retribution for my sin? You shall not take her! I will die first!

JOHN WILSON: (with kindness) My poor woman, the child shall be well cared for—far better than you can do.

HESTER: God gave her into my keeping. I will not give her up! (crying out to Arthur Dimmesdale) Master Dimmesdale, speak for me! You were my pastor, and had charge of my soul, and know me better than these men can. I will not lose the child! Speak for me! You know, for you have sympathies which these men lack! You know what is in my heart, and what are a mother's rights, and how much the stronger they are, when that mother has but her child and the scarlet letter! Look to it! I will not lose the child! Look to it!

ARTHUR DIMMESDALE: (with a sweet, powerful voice) There is truth in what Hester says, and in the feeling which inspires her! God gave her the child, and gave her, too, an instinctive knowledge of its nature and requirements—both seemingly so peculiar—which no other mortal being can possess. And, moreover, is there not a quality of awful sacredness in the relationship between this mother and this child?

GOVERNOR BELLINGHAM: Ay! How is that good, Master Dimmesdale? Make it plain.

ARTHUR DIMMESDALE: It must be so. For, if we deem it otherwise, do we not thereby say that the Heavenly Father, the Creator of all flesh, has lightly recognized a deed of sin and made of no account the distinction between unhallowed lust and holy love? This child of its father's guilt and its mother's shame has come from the hand of God, to work in many ways upon her heart, who pleads so earnestly and with such bitterness of spirit, the right to keep her. It was meant for a blessing, for the one blessing of her life! It was meant, doubtless, as the mother herself has told us, for a retribution too; a torture to be felt at many an unthought-of moment; a pang, a sting, an ever-recurring agony, in the midst of a troubled joy!

Has she not expressed this thought in the garb of the poor child, so forcibly reminding us of that red symbol which sears her bosom?

JOHN WILSON: Well said, again. I feared the woman had no better thought than to make a rebel of her child!

ARTHUR DIMMESDALE: Oh, not so! Not so! She recognizes, believe me, the solemn miracle which God hath wrought, in the existence of that child. And may she feel, too—what, I think, is the very truth—that this boon was meant, above all things else, to keep the mother's soul alive, and to preserve her from blacker depths of sin into which Satan might else have sought to plunge her! Therefore, it is good for this poor, sinful woman that she has an infant immortality, a being capable of eternal joy or sorrow, confided to her care, to be trained up by her to righteousness, to remind her, at every moment, of her fall, but yet to teach her, as it were by the Creator's sacred pledge, that, if she bring the child to heaven, the child also will bring its parent thither! Herein is the sinful mother happier than the sinful father. For Hester Prynne's sake then, and no less for the poor child's sake, let us leave them as Providence has seen fit to place them!

ROGER CHILLINGWORTH: (smiling) Master Dimmesdale, my friend, you speak with a strange earnestness.

JOHN WILSON: And there is a weighty import in what my young brother has spoken. What say you, worshipful Master Bellingham? Has he not pleaded well for the poor woman?

GOVERNOR BELLINGHAM: Indeed he has, and we will leave the matter as it now stands.

NARRATOR: The governor may leave the matter as it now stands, but the characters of the four people—Hester, her husband, Pearl, and Pearl's father—have far to go. Hester will grow stronger; Roger Chillingworth will become more sinister; Pearl will develop into a compassionate woman; and the secret kept too long by Pearl's father will destroy him.

SCRIPTING NOTES

1. The governor's opening lines have been adapted to make it clear that it is the brilliantly dressed Pearl to whom he refers.

2. Words not familiar to a contemporary listening audience have been changed. For example, pray instead of prithee and dressed instead of bedizen have been used as well as substitutions for the pronouns thee, thou, and thy.

3. To maintain the attention of the listening audience, some of the long descriptive dialogue has been omitted (e.g., that in John Wilson's first lines).

RIP VAN WINKLE

Washington Irving

The script is taken from the second half of the story.

STAGING

The narrator stands at a lectern; all other characters sit on stools.

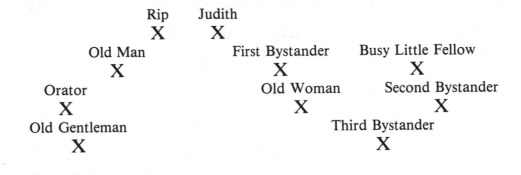

NARRATOR: This script is taken from the classic American short story "Rip Van Winkle" by Washington Irving. The characters are Rip, an obedient henpecked husband and a good-natured neighbor ready to attend to anybody's business but his own, read by _____; the village orator, read by _____; the busy little fellow, read by _____; the old gentleman, read by _____; the old man, read by _____; the old woman, read by _____; Judith Gardenier, the daughter whom Rip has not seen for twenty years, read by _____; and the three bystanders, read by _____, _____, and _____. I, _____, am the narrator.

This scene opens on the morning that Rip Van Winkle has awakened from his twenty-year nap. Nothing is as he remembers it. His doubt and confusion grow as he finds his dog is missing, his house is in decay, the old village inn is gone, and not one familiar face greets him as he wanders into the village. He is dreading to meet his tart-tempered wife, but it would not do to starve alone among the mountains.

Muttering to himself, he approaches a crowd of villagers who have gathered on election day.

RIP:	(muttering to himself) What excuse shall I make to my wife Dame Van Winkle? I shall have a blessed time with her.
THE ENTIRE CROWD:	(eyes Rip from head to foot with great curiosity)
ORATOR:	On which side do you vote?
RIP:	(stares with vacant stupidity)
BUSY LITTLE FELLOW:	Are you Federal or Democrat?
OLD GENTLEMAN:	(with self-importance) What has brought you to the election with a gun on your shoulder? Do you mean to breed a riot in the village?
RIP:	(dismayed) Alas, gentlemen! I am a poor, quiet man, a native of the place, and a loyal subject of the King, God bless him!
BYSTANDER ONE:	(shouting) A tory!
BYSTANDER TWO:	(shouting) A tory! A spy!
BYSTANDER THREE:	(shouting) A refugee! Hustle him!
BYSTANDER ONE:	(shouting) Hustle him!
BYSTANDER TWO:	(shouting) Away with him!
OLD GENTLEMAN:	(holding one hand up in a gesture to calm the crowd) Quiet! Here, here! Quiet! Stranger, I demand that you explain immediately why you are here and whom you are seeking.
RIP:	Sir, I assure you I mean no harm. I am merely looking for my neighbors.
OLD GENTLEMAN:	Well, who are they? Name them.
RIP:	(touching the forehead as in thought) Where's Nicholas Vedder?
OLD MAN:	Nicholas Vedder? Why, he is dead and gone these eighteen years. There *was* a wooden tombstone in the churchyard that used to tell all about him, but that's rotten and gone, too.
RIP:	Where's Brom Dutcher?
OLD MAN:	He went off to the wars, too; was a great militia general, and is now in Congress.

RIP:	(in despair) Does nobody here know Rip Van Winkle?
BYSTANDERS TWO AND THREE:	(exclaim together) Oh, Rip Van Winkle!
BYSTANDER ONE:	Oh, to be sure! That's young Rip Van Winkle yonder, leaning against the tree.
OLD MAN:	Who are you and what is your name?
RIP:	Well—that looks like me. But if that's me, who am I? God knows! I'm not myself—I'm somebody else—that's me yonder—no—that's somebody else, got into my shoes—I was myself last night, but I feel asleep on the mountains, and they've changed my gun, and everything's changed, and I'm changed, and I can't tell what's my name, or who I am!
BYSTANDERS ONE, TWO, AND THREE:	(look at each other, wink, nod, and tap fingers against foreheads)
RIP:	What is *your* name, my good woman?
JUDITH GARDENIER:	Judith Gardenier.
RIP:	And your father's name?
JUDITH GARDENIER:	Ah, poor man, Rip Van Winkle was his name, but it's twenty years since he went away from home with his gun and never has been heard of since—his dog came home without him; but whether he shot himself, or was carried away by the Indians, nobody can tell. I was then but a little girl.
RIP:	(with faltering voice) Where's your mother?
JUDITH GARDENIER:	Oh, she, too, died but a short time since; she broke a blood-vessel in a fit of passion at a New England peddler.
RIP:	(clearly finding comfort in the news about Dame Van Winkle and unable to contain emotion any longer) I am your father! Young Rip Van Winkle once—old Rip Van Winkle now. Does nobody know poor Rip Van Winkle?
OLD WOMAN:	(steps forward from among the bystanders) Sure enough! It is Rip Van Winkle—it is himself. Welcome home again, old neighbor. Why, where have you been all these twenty long years?

NARRATOR: Rip's story was soon told, for the whole twenty years had been to him but as one night; and almost universally the old Dutch inhabitants gave it full credit. To make a long story short, Rip's daughter took him home to live with her. Having nothing to do at home, and having arrived at that happy age when a man is expected to be idle, he took his place once more on the bench at the inn door, and was reverenced as one of the patriarchs of the village and a chronicler of the old times "before the war." As for Rip's son and heir, the young man who was seen leaning against the tree, he was employed to work on the farm, but evinced an hereditary disposition to attend to anything else but his business.

SCRIPTING NOTES

1. Although it is generally recommended that scenes for scripting be taken from the earlier parts of a work, this story is an exception because the outcome is well-known.

2. The old gentleman addresses Rip as stranger in order to define how the crowd views him.

3. An arbitrary decision determined the number of bystanders and the assignment of their lines.

4. After Old Rip saw Young Rip, Old Rip's lines were adapted to include, "Well, that looks like me." That addition was made to communicate the similarity that the text makes clear.

WHITE FANG

Jack London

This script was taken from part I, "The She-Wolf."

STAGING
The narrator stands at a lectern; Bill and Henry sit on stools.

Bill   Henry
X   X

Narrator
X

NARRATOR: This script has been adapted from *White Fang* by Jack London. The characters in this scene are Henry, a tough and determined dogsled driver, read by _____; Bill, Henry's emotional partner, read by _____; and I, _____, the narrator.

Henry and Bill have been driving six sled dogs across the savage, frozen Northland Wild. However, the bitter cold is not as fierce as the pack of wolves which has been following them and which has already by some means taken one dog away to be devoured. On this particular morning, as well as the one that follows, the men begin their day by feeding the dogs and making their own breakfast. It is dark, and the temperature is fifty below.

HENRY: (calling out) Hello! What's up with the dogs.

BILL: (with anger and exasperation) Another dog is gone. Frog's gone.

HENRY: (with disbelief) No.

BILL: I tell you yes. (pause, then without emotion) Frog was the strongest dog of the bunch.

HENRY: An' he was no fool dog neither. (gloomily) We've lost two dogs in two days.

NARRATOR: The men harness the remaining four dogs and drive them until darkness comes in the middle of the afternoon, and then they make camp. To hold the dogs, Bill ties them, using a combination of long sticks and leather thongs.

HENRY:	(nodding approvingly) It's the only contraption that'll ever hold One Ear. He can gnaw through leather as clean as a knife an' jes' about half as quick. They all'll be here in the mornin' hunkydory.
BILL:	You jes' bet they will. If one of 'em turns up missin', I'll go without my coffee.
HENRY:	Those wolves jes' know we ain't loaded to kill. If we could put a couple of shots into 'em, they'd be more respectful. They come closer every night. Look! There! Get the firelight out of your eyes an' look hard—there! Did you see that wolf?
BILL AND HENRY:	(both men peer to the left)
HENRY:	(whispering) Look at that, Bill.
BILL:	(in a low tone) That fool dog One Ear don't seem scairt much what with that whining and eagerness to be free.
HENRY:	(whispering) It's a she-wolf, an' that accounts for Fatty an' Frog. She's the decoy for the pack. She draws out the dog an' then all the rest pitches in an' eats 'm up.
BILL:	Henry, I'm thinkin'.
HENRY:	Thinkin' what?
BILL:	I'm a-thinkin' that was the extra dog that I lambasted with the club at feeding time yesterday.
HENRY:	Ain't the slightest doubt in the world.
BILL:	An' right here I want to remark that that animal's familiarity with campfires is suspicious an' immoral.
HENRY:	It knows for certain more'n a self-respectin' wolf ought to know. A wolf that knows enough to come in with the dogs at feedin' time has had experiences.
BILL:	(thinking out loud) Ol' Villan had a dog once that run away with the wolves. I ought to know. I shot it out of the pack in a moose pasture over on Little Stick. An' Ol' Villan cried like a baby. Hadn't seen it for three years, he said. Been with the wolves all that time.
HENRY:	I reckon you've called the turn, Bill. That wolf's a dog, an' it's eaten fish many's the time from the hand of man.
BILL:	An' if I get a chance at it, that wolf that's a dog'll be jes' meat. We can't afford to lose no more animals.

HENRY:	But you've only got three cartridges.
BILL:	I'll wait for a dead sure shot.
NARRATOR:	In the morning Henry renewed the fire and cooked breakfast to the accompaniment of his partner's snoring.
HENRY:	You was sleepin' jes' too comfortable for anythin'. I hadn't the heart to rouse you.
BILL:	(gently chiding) This breakfast's mighty fine, but where's my coffee?
HENRY:	(shaking his head) You don't get no coffee.
BILL:	(anxiously) Ain't run out?
HENRY:	Nope.
BILL:	Ain't thinkin' it'll hurt my digestion?
HENRY:	Nope.
BILL:	(angrily) Then it's jes' warm an' anxious I am to be hearin' you explain yourself.
HENRY:	Spanker's gone.
BILL:	(apathetically) How'd it happen?
HENRY:	Don't know. Unless One Ear gnawed 'm loose. He couldn't a-done it himself, that's sure.
BILL:	The darned cuss. Jes' because he couldn't chew himself loose, he chews Spanker loose.
HENRY:	Well, Spanker's troubles is over, anyway; I guess he's digested by this time an' cavortin' over the landscape in the bellies of twenty different wolves. Have some coffee, Bill.
BILL:	(shakes his head)
HENRY:	(pleading) Go on.
BILL:	I'll be ding-dong-danged if I do. I said I wouldn't if ary dog turned up missin', an' I won't.
HENRY:	(enticingly) It's darn good coffee.
BILL:	I'll tie 'em up out of reach of each other tonight.
NARRATOR:	The two men harness the dogs and travel little more than a hundred yards, when Henry bends down and picks up something. He recognizes it. It is all that is left of Spanker—the stick with which he had been tied.

HENRY:	Mebbe you'll need that in your business.
BILL:	(shaken) They ate 'm hide an' all. The stick's as clean as a whistle. They've ate the leather offen both ends. They're hungry, Henry, an' they'll have you an' me guessin' before this trip's over.
HENRY:	(laughing defiantly) I ain't been trailed this way by wolves before, but I've gone through a whole lot worse an' kept my health. Takes more'n a handful of them pesky critters to do for yours truly, Bill, my son.
BILL:	(muttering ominously) I don't know, I don't know.
NARRATOR:	Bill does know only too well the danger that hunts them, and it is Kiche, part wolf and part dog, who survives the famine and later gives birth to White Fang. Both Kiche and White Fang will come to live in the world of humans, and the story that unfolds is the tale of White Fang's life under the harshest of masters and later under the kindest of masters. In both cases White Fang—like his mother Kiche— will live the drama of the survival of the fittest.

SCRIPTING NOTES

1. This scene requires an adaptation that makes clear that Spanker, Frog, and One Ear are dogs.

2. The fact that Bill and Henry were looking at the she-wolf when they peered into the darkness was incorporated into their dialogue.

THE PURLOINED LETTER

Edgar Allan Poe

The script is taken from the first half of the story.

STAGING
The narrator stands at a lectern; the other characters sit in chairs.

The Prefect
X

Dupin   Dupin's Friend
X   X

Narrator
X

NARRATOR: The scene that we are sharing is from Edgar Allan Poe's short story "The Purloined Letter." The readers for this scene are _____, reading the character of C. Auguste Dupin, a brilliant Parisian detective; _____, reading the character of Dupin's admiring friend; _____, reading the character of their baffled old acquaintance, the Prefect of the Parisian Police, whom they find both entertaining and contemptible; and I, _____, the narrator.

The setting for this scene is nineteenth-century Paris. Dupin and his friend are enjoying a quiet autumn evening in Dupin's library when unexpectedly the Prefect of the police drops by. They give the Prefect a hearty welcome and offer him a comfortable chair, but they smugly assume that a troublesome case has caused the Prefect to seek Monsieur Dupin's advice.

FRIEND: And what is the difficulty now?

THE PREFECT: (attempting to disguise his embarrassment) The fact is, the business is *very* simple indeed, and I make no doubt that we can manage it sufficiently well ourselves; but then I thought Dupin would like to hear the details of it because it is so excessively *odd*.

DUPIN: (somewhat amused) Simple and odd.

THE PREFECT: Why, yes, and not exactly that either. The fact is, we have all been a good deal puzzled because the affair *is* so simple, and yet baffles us altogether.

DUPIN: Perhaps it is the very simplicity of the thing which puts you at fault.

THE PREFECT: (laughing heartily) What nonsense you *do* talk!

DUPIN: Perhaps the mystery is a little *too* plain.

THE PREFECT: Oh, good heavens! Who ever heard of such an idea?

DUPIN: (with a hint of sarcasm) A little *too* self-evident.

THE PREFECT: (roaring with amusement) Ha! Ha! Ha! Ha! Ha! Ha! Ho! Ho! Ho! Oh, Dupin, you will be the death of me yet!

FRIEND: And what, after all, *is* the matter on hand?

THE PREFECT: Why, I will tell you. (settles more comfortably into his chair) I will tell you in a few words; but, before I begin, let me caution you that this is an affair demanding the greatest secrecy, (in a stage whisper) and that I should most probably lose the position I now hold, were it known that I confided it to any one.

FRIEND: Proceed.

DUPIN: (aloofly) Or not.

THE PREFECT: Well then, I have received personal information, from a very high quarter, that a certain document of the most importance has been purloined from the royal apartments. The individual who purloined it is known; this beyond a doubt; he was seen to take it. It is known, also, that it still remains in his possession, and upon this conviction I proceeded. My first care was to make thorough search of the minister's hotel, and here my chief embarrassment lay in the necessity of searching without his knowledge. Beyond all things, I have been warned of the danger which would result from giving him reason to suspect our design.

FRIEND: But you are quite accomplished in these investigations. The Parisian police have done this thing often before.

THE PREFECT: Oh, yes, and for this reason I did not despair. The habits of the minister gave me, too, a great advantage. He is frequently absent from home all night. His servants are by no means numerous. They sleep at a distance from their master's apartment, and, being chiefly Neapolitans, are readily made drunk. I have keys, as you know, with which I can open any chamber in Paris. For three months a night has not passed, during the greater part of which I have not been engaged, personally, in ransacking the hotel. My honor is interested, and, to mention a great secret, the reward is enormous. So I did not abandon the search until I had become fully satisfied that the thief is a more astute man than myself. I fancy that I have investigated every nook and corner of the premises in which it is possible that the paper can be concealed.

FRIEND: But is it not possible that although the letter may be in possession of the minister, as it unquestionably is, he may have concealed it elsewhere than upon his own premises?

DUPIN: This is barely possible. The present peculiar condition of affairs at court, and especially of those intrigues in which the minister is known to be involved, would render the instant availability of the document — its susceptibility of being produced at a moment's notice — a point of nearly equal importance with its possession.

FRIEND: Its susceptibility of being produced?

DUPIN: That is to say, of being *destroyed.*

FRIEND: True. The paper is clearly then upon the premises. As for its being upon the person of the minister, we may consider that as out of the question.

THE PREFECT: Entirely. He has been twice waylaid, as if by footpads, and his person rigidly searched under my own inspection.

DUPIN: You might have spared yourself this trouble. The minister, I presume, is not altogether a fool, and, if not, must have anticipated these waylayings as a matter of course.

THE PREFECT: (with naive sarcasm) Not *altogether* a fool, but then he is a poet, which I take to be only one removed from a fool.

DUPIN: (with a hint of irony) True, although I have been guilty of certain doggerel myself.

FRIEND: Suppose you detail the particulars of your search.

THE PREFECT: Why, the fact is, we took our time, and we searched *everywhere.* I have had long experience in these affairs. I took the entire building, room by room; devoting the nights of a whole week to each. We examined, first, the furniture of each apartment. We opened every possible drawer; and I presume you know that, to a properly trained police agent, such a thing as a *secret* drawer is impossible. Any man is a dolt who permits a secret drawer to escape him in a search of this kind. The thing is *so* plain. There is a certain amount of bulk — of space — to be accounted for in every cabinet. Then we have accurate rules. The fiftieth part of line could not escape us. After the cabinets we took the chairs. The cushions we probed with the fine long needles you have seen me employ. From the tables we removed the tops.

FRIEND: Why so?

THE PREFECT: Sometimes the top of a table, or other similarly arranged piece of furniture, is removed by the person wishing to conceal an article; then the leg is excavated, the article deposited within the cavity, and the top replaced. The bottoms and tops of bedposts are employed in the same way.

FRIEND: But could not the cavity be detected by sounding?

THE PREFECT: By no means, if, when the article is deposited, a sufficient wadding of cotton be placed around it. Besides, in our case, we were obliged to proceed without noise.

FRIEND: But you could not have removed — you could not have taken to pieces *all* articles of furniture in which it would have been possible to make a deposit in the manner you mention. A letter may be compressed into a thin spiral roll, not differing much in shape or bulk from a large knitting needle, and in this form it might be inserted into the rung of a chair, for example. You did not take to pieces all the chairs?

THE PREFECT: Certainly not; but we did better — we examined the rungs of every chair in the hotel, and indeed, the jointings of every description of furniture, by the aid of a most powerful microscope. Had there been any traces of recent disturbance, we should not have failed to detect it instantly. A single grain of gimlet dust, for example, would have been as obvious as an apple. Any disorder in the gluing — any unusual gaping in the joints — would have sufficed to insure detection.

FRIEND: I presume you looked to the mirrors, between the boards and the plates, and you probed the beds and the bedclothes, as well as the curtains and carpets.

THE PREFECT: That of course; and when we had absolutely completed every particle of the furniture in this way, then we examined the house itself. We divided its entire surface into compartments, which we numbered so that none might be missed; then we scrutinized each individual square inch throughout the premises, including the two houses immediately adjoining, with the microscope as before.

FRIEND: (exclaiming) The two houses adjoining? You must have had a great deal of trouble.

THE PREFECT: We had, but the reward offered is prodigious.

FRIEND: You included the *grounds* about the houses?

THE PREFECT: All the grounds are paved with brick. They gave us comparatively little trouble. We examined the moss between the bricks and found it undisturbed.

FRIEND: You looked among the minister's papers, of course, and into the books of the library?

THE PREFECT: Certainly, we opened every package and parcel. We not only opened every book, but we turned over every leaf in each volume, not contenting ourselves with a mere shake, according to the fashion of some police officers. We also measured the thickness of every book *cover* with the most accurate measurement, and applied to each the most zealous scrutiny of the microscope. Had any of the bindings been recently meddled with, it would have been utterly impossible that the fact should have escaped observation.

FRIEND: You explored the floors beneath the carpets?

THE PREFECT: Beyond doubt. We removed every carpet, and examined the boards with the microscope.

FRIEND: And the paper on the walls?

THE PREFECT: Yes.

FRIEND: You looked into the cellars?

THE PREFECT: We did.

FRIEND: Then, you have been making a miscalculation, and the letter is *not* upon the premises, as you suppose.

THE PREFECT: I fear you are right there. And now, Dupin, what would you advise me to do?

NARRATOR: Thus, with the Parisian police baffled, Monsieur C. Auguste Dupin is given another opportunity to display his remarkable skills as an investigator.

SCRIPTING NOTES
1. This story is written from the first-person point of view of the friend. His thoughts and interpretations were incorporated into the narrator's lines.

2. The lengthy explanation of how the letter was stolen was omitted, thus leading the audience straight to the puzzle laid before Dupin.

3. The readers for the characters of Dupin and his friend may need special coaching in order to communicate the feeling that the two find the Prefect both entertaining and slightly contemptible.

FRANKENSTEIN
Mary W. Shelley

This script is taken from chapter 15.

STAGING

The narrator stands at a lectern; the monster and DeLacey sit in chairs.

The Monster   DeLacey

X   X

Narrator

X

NARRATOR: The script that we are sharing is from *Frankenstein* by Mary W. Shelley. The characters are the lonely monster, read by _____; a blind old gentleman, DeLacey, read by _____; and I, _____, the narrator.

This particular scene occurs when the monster, Victor Frankenstein's creation, is one year old. Because the monster has terrified everyone he has met, he has spent the last several months hiding. However, he has taken a great interest in the DeLacey household, and he has quietly observed them, learning their ways and language. He has been touched by their affection for each other, and he has secretly shoveled snow, stacked firewood, and performed other kindnesses for them. Because he has never seen them drive away the poor that have stopped at their door, he hopes that they will accept him. The father of the household is DeLacey, and the monster plans to win the family's affection by first telling his story to the blind DeLacey. Therefore, one day when the other members of the household have gone for a country walk, the monster knocks at DeLacey's cottage door.

DELACEY: (friendly) Who is there? Come in.

THE MONSTER: (politely) Pardon this intrusion; I am a traveler in want of a little rest. You would greatly oblige me if you would allow me to remain a few minutes before the fire.

DELACEY: Enter, and I will try in what manner I can to relieve your wants. But, unfortunately, my children are away from home. And as I am blind, I am afraid I shall find it difficult to procure food for you.

THE MONSTER: Do not trouble yourself, my kind host. I have food. It is warmth and rest only that I need.

DELACEY: By your language, stranger, I suppose you are my countryman. Are you French?

THE MONSTER: No, but I was educated by a French family and understand that language only. I am now going to claim the protection of some friends, whom I sincerely love, and of whose favour I have some hopes.

DELACEY: (interested) Are they Germans?

THE MONSTER: No, they are French. But let us change the subject. I am an unfortunate and deserted creature. I look around and I have no relation or friend upon earth. These amiable people to whom I go have never seen me and know little of me. I am full of fears, for if I fail there, I am an outcast in the world forever.

DELACEY: (kindly) Do not despair. To be friendless is indeed to be unfortunate, but the hearts of men, when unprejudiced by any obvious self-interest, are full of brotherly love and charity. Rely, therefore, on your hopes; and if these friends are good and amiable, do not despair.

THE MONSTER: They are kind—they are the most excellent creatures in the world; but, unfortunately, they are prejudiced against me. I have good dispositions. My life has been hitherto harmless and in some degree beneficial, but a fatal prejudice clouds their eyes, and where they ought to see a feeling and kind friend, they behold only a detestable monster.

DELACEY: That is indeed unfortunate; but if you are really blameless, cannot you undeceive them?

THE MONSTER: I am about to undertake that task, and it is on that account that I feel so many overwhelming terrors. I tenderly love these friends. I have, unknown to them, been for many months in the habits of daily kindness towards them; but they believe that I wish to injure them, and it is that prejudice which I wish to overcome.

DELACEY: Where do these friends reside?

THE MONSTER: Near this spot.

DELACEY: If you will unreservedly confide to me the particulars of your tale, I perhaps may be of use in undeceiving them. I am blind and cannot judge of your countenance, but there is something in your words which persuades me that you are sincere. I am poor and an exile, but it will afford me true pleasure to be in any way serviceable to a human creature.

THE MONSTER: (thankfully) Excellent man! I thank you and accept your generous offer. You raise me from the dust by this kindness; and I trust that, by your aid, I shall not be driven from the society and sympathy of your fellow creatures.

DELACEY: Heaven forbid! Even if you were really criminal, for that can only drive you to desperation, and not instigate you to virtue. I also am unfortunate. I and my family have been condemned, although innocent. Judge, therefore, if I do not feel for your misfortunes.

THE MONSTER: How can I thank you, my best and only benefactor? From your lips first have I heard the voice of kindness directed towards me; I shall be forever grateful; and your present humanity assures me of success with those friends whom I am on the point of meeting.

DELACEY: May I know the names and residence of those friends?

THE MONSTER: (surprised) I hear your family coming! (pleading with great emotion) Now is the time! Save and protect me! You and your family are the friends whom I seek. Do not you desert me in the hour of trial!

DELACEY: (shocked) Great God! Who are you?

NARRATOR: At that instant the cottage door was opened, and Felix, Safie, and Agatha entered. Who can describe their horror and consternation on beholding the monster? Agatha, the daughter, fainted; and Safie, unable to attend to her friend, rushed out of the cottage. Felix, the son, darted forward and with supernatural force tore the monster from his father, to whose knees he clung. In a transport of fury, Felix dashed the monster to the ground and struck him. The monster could have torn Felix limb from limb, as the lion rends the antelope. But the monster's heart sank within him as with bitter sickness, and he refrained. The monster saw Felix on the point of repeating his blow, when, overcome by pain and anguish, he quitted the cottage and in the general tumult escaped unperceived to his hovel. Thus, driven from society to be an outcast in the world forever, the monster felt only great bitterness toward humankind and especially toward his creator, Victor Frankenstein.

SCRIPTING NOTES

1. This first-person account by the monster to Victor Frankenstein has been adapted so that the narrator not only introduces and closes the script, but also provides insight into the thoughts of the monster.

2. Excluding the narrator's opening and closing lines, this script flows word for word from the novel's text.

THE STRANGE CASE OF
DR. JEKYLL AND MR. HYDE
Robert Louis Stevenson

This script is taken from the chapter "Dr. Jekyll Was Quite at Ease."

STAGING
The narrator stands at a lectern; the other characters sit in chairs.

Mr. Utterson   Dr. Jekyll

X   X

Narrator

X

NARRATOR: This script has been adapted from Robert Louis Stevenson's *Dr. Jekyll and Mr. Hyde*. The characters in this scene are Dr. Jekyll, a man respected by his friends, read by _____; Mr. Utterson, Dr. Jekyll's old friend and trusted lawyer, read by _____. I, _____, am the narrator.

The setting for this story is nineteenth-century London. In this scene Mr. Utterson, worried about the well-being of Dr. Jekyll, has lingered after a dinner party so that he may talk to him. The concern centers around two facts: Dr. Jekyll has mysteriously made a certain Mr. Hyde the sole heir of his will, and Mr. Hyde is known to be a sinister man who has been seen calmly trampling a child on the street. Mr. Utterson has imagined the ghost of some old sin is forcing Dr. Jekyll to meet demands by Mr. Hyde, and he fears that Dr. Jekyll's life is endangered.

MR. UTTERSON: (with gravity) Jekyll, I have been wanting to speak to you. You know that will of yours?

DR. JEKYLL: (attempting to appear in good humor) My poor Utterson, you are unfortunate in such a client. I never saw a man so distressed as you were by my will.

MR. UTTERSON: You know I never approved of it.

DR. JEKYLL: (sharply) My will? Yes, certainly, I know that. You have told me so.

MR. UTTERSON: Well, I tell you so again. I have been learning something of young Hyde.

DR. JEKYLL: (coldly) I do not care to hear more. This is a matter I thought we had agreed to drop.

MR. UTTERSON: What I heard was abominable.

DR. JEKYLL: (somewhat confusedly) It can make no change. You do not understand my position. I am painfully situated. Utterson, my position is a very strange — a very strange one. It is one of those affairs that cannot be mended by talking.

MR. UTTERSON: (earnestly) Jekyll, you know me: I am a man to be trusted. Make a clean breast of this in confidence, and I make no doubt I can get you out of it.

DR. JEKYLL: (reasonably) I have no doubt you are perfectly right. (pausing) Well, but since we have touched upon this business, and for the last time, I hope, there is one point I should like you to understand. I have really a very great interest in poor Hyde. I know you have seen him. He told me so, and I fear he was rude. But I do sincerely take a great, a very great interest in that young man; and if I am taken away, Utterson, I wish you to promise me that you will bear with him and get his rights for him. I think you would, if you knew all; and it would be a weight off my mind if you would promise.

MR. UTTERSON: (frankly) I can't pretend that I shall ever like him.

DR. JEKYLL: (pleading) I don't ask that. I only ask for justice; I only ask you to help him for my sake, when I am no longer here.

MR. UTTERSON: (sighing) Well, I promise.

NARRATOR: The mystery that binds Dr. Jekyll and Mr. Hyde is beyond Mr. Utterson's imagination, and his pledge of justice and help falls short of any hope of fulfillment. Dr. Jekyll and Mr. Hyde have set their own course — a course both deadly and unalterable.

SCRIPTING NOTES

1. Dr. Jekyll's comments about events surrounding Mr. Lanyon (who would be unknown to a listening audience) have been omitted.

2. This brief script was developed almost word for word from the original text.

A CONNECTICUT YANKEE IN KING ARTHUR'S COURT

Mark Twain

This script is taken from chapter 17, "A Royal Banquet."

STAGING

The narrator stands at a lectern; the queen and the minister sit on stools, the prisoner and his wife sit in chairs.

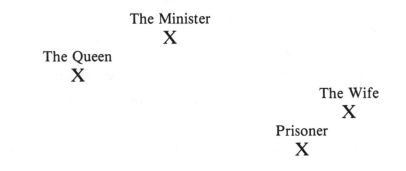

The Minister
X

The Queen
X

The Wife
X

Prisoner
X

Narrator
X

NARRATOR: The script that we are sharing is from Mark Twain's satirical fantasy *A Connecticut Yankee in King Arthur's Court*. The readers are _____, reading the part of the single-minded queen; _____, reading the part of the perplexed minister; _____, reading the part of the tortured prisoner; and _____, reading the part of the prisoner's wife. I, _____, am the narrator.

The premise behind this fantasy is that a nineteenth-century mechanic, in the process of losing a fight, was knocked unconscious by a blow from a crow bar. He awakens in King Arthur's Camelot. Through his understanding of nineteenth-century science, he has passed himself off as a magician, and he has bargained for a position as King Arthur's minister.

In this scene, the mechanic—now minister—and the queen are chatting after a banquet. The queen is a master talker, and her silver bell of a tongue tinkles along in the otherwise profound and ghostly hush of the sleeping castle until by and by there comes, as if from deep down under them, a far-away sound, as of a muffled shriek—with an expression of agony about it that makes the minister's flesh crawl.

QUEEN: (The queen smiles. Her eyes light with pleasure. Cupping her hand behind her ear, she tilts her head as a bird does when it listens.)

MINISTER: (shocked with horror) What is it?

QUEEN: (matter-of-factly) It is truly a stubborn soul, and endureth long. It is many hours now.

MINISTER: Endureth what?

QUEEN: (happily) The rack. Come—ye shall see a blithe sight. And he yield not his secret now, ye shall see him torn asunder.

NARRATOR: The queen and the minister, conducted by mailed guard bearing flaring torches, tramp along echoing corridors and down stone stairways dank and dripping and smelling of mould and ages of imprisoned night. It is a long journey, and not made the shorter by the queen's explanation of the prisoner and his crime. He has been accused by an anonymous informer of having killed a stag in the royal preserves.

MINISTER: Anonymous testimony isn't just the right thing, your Highness. It were fairer to confront the accused with the accuser.

QUEEN: (cheerily) I had not thought of that, it being but of small consequence. But if I would, I could not, for that the accuser came masked by night and told the forester, and straightway got him hence again, and so the forester knoweth him not.

MINISTER: (puzzled) Then is the Unknown the only person who saw the stag killed?

QUEEN: Marry, *no* man *saw* the killing, but this Unknown saw this hardy wretch near to the spot where the stag lay and came with right loyal zeal and betrayed him to the forester.

MINISTER: So the Unknown was near the dead stag, too? Isn't it just possible that he did the killing himself? His loyal zeal—in a mask—looks just a shade suspicious. But what is your Highness's idea for racking the prisoner? Where is the profit?

QUEEN: He will not confess, else, and then were his soul lost. For his crime his life is forfeited by the law—and of a surety will I see that he payeth it! But it were peril to my own soul to let him die unconfessed and unabsolved. Nay, I were a fool to fling me into hell for *his* accommodation.

MINISTER: But, your Highness, suppose he has nothing to confess?

QUEEN: As to that, we shall see, anon. If I rack him to death and he confess not, it will peradventure show that he had indeed naught to confess—ye will grant that that is sooth? Then shall I not be damned for an unconfessed man that had naught to confess—wherefore, I shall be safe.

MINISTER: (looking up at the ceiling, he slowly shakes his head, resigned that it is useless to argue with her)

NARRATOR: At this point the queen and the minister enter the rack cell, and the minister approaches the prisoner.

MINISTER: Now, my friend, tell me your side of this matter. I know the other side.

PRISONER: (Refusing to speak, he shakes his head.)

MINISTER: You know of me?

PRISONER: Yes. All do, in Arthur's realms.

MINISTER: If my reputation has come to you right and straight, you should not be afraid to speak.

WIFE: (pleading) Ah, fair my lord, do thou persuade him! Thou canst and thou wilt. Ah, he suffereth so, and it is for me—for *me*! And how can I bear it? I would I might see him die—a sweet, swift death. Oh, my husband, I cannot bear this one!

PRISONER: Peace! Wife, you know not what ye ask. Shall I starve you, whom I love, to win a gentle death? I wish thou knewest me better.

MINISTER: (obviously puzzled) Well, I can't quite make this out. Is it a puzzle. Now—

WIFE: (eagerly) Ah, dear, my dear minister, and ye will but persuade him! Consider how these his tortures wound me! Oh, and he will not speak! Whereas, the healing, the solace that lie in a blessed swift death—

MINISTER: (slightly irritated) What *are* you maundering about? He's going out from here a free man and whole—he's not going to die.

PRISONER: (His face lights up.)

WIFE: (in an explosion of joy) He is saved! For it is the king's word by the mouth of the king's minister. Arthur, the king whose word is gold!

MINISTER: Well, then you do believe I can be trusted, after all. Why didn't you before?

PRISONER: Who doubted? Not I, indeed, and not she.

MINISTER: Well, why wouldn't you tell me your story, then?

PRISONER: Ye had made no promise, else had it been otherwise.

MINISTER: I see, I see ... and yet I believe I don't quite see, after all. You stood the torture and refused to confess, which shows plain enough to even the dullest understanding that you had nothing to confess—

PRISONER: (surprised) *I*, my lord? How so? It was I that killed the deer!

MINISTER: (amazed) You *did*? Oh, dear, this is the most mixed-up business that ever—

WIFE: (interrupting) Dear lord, I begged him on my knees to confess.

MINISTER: (confounded) You *did*! It gets thicker and thicker. What did you want him to do that for?

WIFE: So that it would bring him a quick death and save him all this cruel pain.

MINISTER: (appearing to understand) Well yes, there is reason in that. But *he* didn't want the quick death.

WIFE: He? Why, of a surety he *did*.

MINISTER: Well, then, why in the world *didn't* he confess?

PRISONER: Ah, sweet sir, and leave my wife and chick without bread and shelter?

MINISTER: Oh, heart of gold, now I see it! The bitter law takes the convicted man's estate and beggars his widow and his orphans. They could torture you to death, but without conviction or confession they could not rob your wife and baby. You stood by them like a man; and *you*—true wife and true woman that you are—you would have bought him release from torture at cost to yourself of slow starvation and death. Well, it humbles a body to think what your sex can do when it comes to self-sacrifice. I'll book you both for my colony. You'll like it there. It's a factory where I'm going to turn groping and grubbing automata into men.

NARRATOR: However, neither the prisoner nor the minister book passage for Hartford, Connecticut. For far longer than the minister imagines, he will remain in the sixth century and observe the flaws and foibles of Camelot, providing Twain many opportunities to satirize church, state, and human nature.

SCRIPTING NOTES

1. Most of the other titles given to the minister (e.g., lord and servant) were replaced with "minister" in order to avoid confusion.

2. The single occasion when the prisoner was addressed by his first name was omitted.

3. In order to maintain the flow of dialogue, the queen's dismissal of guards in the rack cell as well as the queen's simultaneous departure were omitted.

4. The narrator's lines were taken from the minister's first-person account in the original text. Therefore, the emotions and thoughts of the minister were implied by delivery and not directly stated.

THE ADVENTURES OF TOM SAWYER

Mark Twain

This script is taken from chapter 9, "Tragedy in the Graveyard."

STAGING

The narrator stands at a lectern; Tom and Huck sit on the floor.

Tom Sawyer   Huck Finn

X   X

Narrator

X

NARRATOR: The script that we will read to you is from Mark Twain's novel *The Adventures of Tom Sawyer*. This scene is from chapter 9, "Tragedy in the Graveyard." The characters in this scene are Tom Sawyer, the all-American boy, read by _____; Huck Finn, the juvenile delinquent of the village, read by _____. I, _____, am the narrator.

The village cemetery at midnight is the setting for this scene. Tom and Huck are waiting in the dark to prove the superstition that throwing a dead cat after an evil ghost will cure warts. Huck has the dead cat, and they have waited for a long time.

TOM: (quietly) Hucky, do you believe the dead people like it for us to be here?

HUCK: (in a stage whisper) I wisht I knowed. It's awful solemn like, *ain't* it?

TOM: I bet it is. (in a stage whisper) Say, Hucky—do you reckon Hoss Williams hears us talking?

HUCK: O' course he does. Least his sperrit does.

TOM: (nervously) I wish I'd said *Mister* Williams. But I never meant any harm. Everybody calls him Hoss.

HUCK: A body can't be too partic'lar how they talk about these yer dead people, Tom.

TOM:	(suddenly) Sh!
HUCK:	What is it, Tom?
TOM:	Sh! There 'tis again! Didn't you hear it?
HUCK:	I—
TOM:	(interrupting) There! Now you hear it.
HUCK:	Lord, Tom, they're coming! They're coming sure. What'll we do?
TOM:	I dono. Think they'll see us?
HUCK:	Oh, Tom, ghosts can see in the dark, same as cats. I wisht I hadn't come.
TOM:	Oh, don't be afeared. *I* don't believe they'll bother us. We ain't doing any harm. If we keep perfectly still, maybe they won't notice us at all.
HUCK:	I'll try to, Tom, but, Lord, I'm all of a shiver.
TOM:	Listen! (in a stage whisper) Look! See there! What is it?
HUCK:	It's devil-fire. Oh, Tom, this is awful.
NARRATOR:	Some vague figures approach through the gloom, swinging an old-fashioned tin lantern that freckles the ground with innumerable little spangles of light.
HUCK:	(shuddering) It's the devils, sure enough. Three of 'em! Lordy, Tom, we're goners! Can you pray?
TOM:	I'll try, but don't you be afeard. They ain't going to hurt us. Now I lay me down to sleep, I—
HUCK:	Sh!
TOM:	What is it, Huck?
HUCK:	They're *humans*! One of 'em is, anyway. One of 'em's old Muff Potter's voice.
TOM:	No—'tain't so, is it?
HUCK:	I bet I know it. Don't you stir nor budge. *He* ain't sharp enough to notice us. Drunk, the same as usual, likely—blamed old rip!
TOM:	All right, I'll keep still. Now they're stuck. Can't find it. Here they come again. Now they're hot. Cold again. Hot again. Red hot! They're p'inted right, this time. Say, Huck, I know another o' them voices; it's Injun Joe.
HUCK:	That's so—that murderer! I'd druther they was devils a dern sight. What kin they be up to?

NARRATOR: "Murderer" was right. What Tom and Huck saw that night left them speechless with horror and flung them into a series of adventures that made Tom the hero of every boy in town.

SCRIPTING NOTES

1. This scene is a good one to demonstrate the showing of emotion (i.e., fear) through voice and tense, shivering body language.

2. The text's long pauses between Tom and Huck's exchanges were omitted because of the need to maintain the audience's involvement.

3. The script does not include the entire chapter because after Injun Joe, Muff Potter, and Dr. Robinson arrive the text involves much action which cannot be reasonably incorporated into dialogue.

4. The readers for the parts of Tom and Huck are directed to sit on the floor to communicate their being "ensconced" among the elms and tombstones.

THE PICTURE OF DORIAN GRAY
Oscar Wilde

This script is taken from chapter 2.

STAGING

The narrator stands at a lectern; the remaining characters sit in chairs.

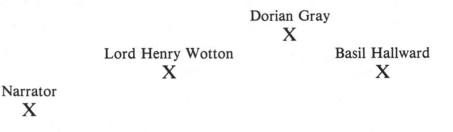

Dorian Gray
X

Lord Henry Wotton Basil Hallward
X X

Narrator
X

NARRATOR: This scene has been adapted from *The Picture of Dorian Gray* by Oscar Wilde. The characters in this scene are Dorian Gray, a handsome and well-liked young man, read by _____; Basil Hallward, an artist who is painting a portrait of Dorian Gray, read by _____; and Lord Henry Wotton, Basil's cynical friend who is known for his destructive influence, read by _____. I, _____, am the narrator.

This scene takes place in Basil's studio as he adds the final touches to Dorian's portrait. Basil has been mysteriously compelled to paint this portrait, and he feels that the simple and beautiful nature of his handsome subject has made this his best work yet. As Dorian sits for Basil, he and Lord Henry carry on a lengthy discussion. Basil is not pleased that Lord Henry Wotton has dropped by, and earlier in the day he had specifically asked Lord Henry not to corrupt his young subject. However, Basil is totally involved with his painting, and throughout the afternoon he is oblivious of the fact that Henry has been lecturing young Dorian on the virtues of selfishness and the values of superficial beauty.

HENRY: Mr. Gray, the gods have been good to you. But what the gods give they quickly take away. You have only a few years in which to live really, perfectly, and fully. When your youth goes, your beauty will go with it, and then you will suddenly discover that there are no triumphs left for you. Every month as it wanes brings you nearer to something dreadful. Time is jealous of you. You will become sallow, and hollow-cheeked, and dull-eyed. You will suffer horribly.... Ah! Realize your youth while you have it. Don't squander the gold of your days, listening to the tedious, trying to improve the hopeless failure, or giving away your life to the ignorant, the common, and the vulgar. These are the sickly aims, the false ideals, of our age. Live! Live the wonderful life that is in you! Let nothing be lost upon you. Be always searching for new sensations. Be afraid of nothing. There is such a little time that your youth will last—such a little time. Youth! Youth! There is absolutely nothing in the world but youth!

BASIL: Ah, finally, the painting is quite finished.

HENRY: My dear fellow, I congratulate you most warmly. It is the finest portrait of modern times. Mr. Gray, come over and look at yourself.

DORIAN: Is it really finished?

BASIL: Quite finished, and you have sat splendidly today. I am awfully obliged to you.

HENRY: That is entirely due to me. Isn't it, Mr. Gray?

BASIL: (following a pause) Dorian, don't you like it?

HENRY: Of course he likes it. Who wouldn't like it? It is one of the greatest things in modern art. I will give you anything you like to ask for it. I must have it.

BASIL: It is not my property, Henry.

HENRY: Whose property is it?

BASIL: Dorian's, of course.

HENRY: He is a very lucky fellow.

DORIAN: (murmuring) How sad it is! How sad it is! I shall grow old, and horrible, and dreadful. But this picture will remain always young. It will never be older than this particular day of June.... If it were only the other way! If it were I who was to be always young, and the picture that was to grow old! For that—for that—I would give everything! Yes, there is nothing in the whole world I would not give! I would give my soul for that!

HENRY: Basil, you would hardly care for such an arrangement. (laughing) It would be rather hard lines on your work.

BASIL: (seriously) I should object very strongly, Henry.

DORIAN: (with contemptible sarcasm) I believe you would, Basil. You like your art better than your friends. I am no more to you than a green bronze figure. Hardly as much, I dare say.

BASIL: (staring in amazement at Dorian)

DORIAN: Yes, I am less to you than your ivory or silver statues. You will like them always. How long will you like me? Till I have my first wrinkle, I suppose. I know, now, that when one loses one's good looks, whatever they may be, one loses everything. Your picture has taught me that. Lord Henry Wotton is perfectly right. Youth is the only thing worth having. When I find that I am growing old, I shall kill myself.

BASIL: Dorian! Dorian! Don't talk like that. I have never had such a friend as you, and I shall never have such another. You are not jealous of material things, are you? You who are finer than any of them!

DORIAN: I am jealous of everything whose beauty does not die. I am jealous of the portrait you have painted of me. Why should it keep what I must lose? Every moment that passes takes something from me, and gives something to it. Oh, if it were only the other way! Why did you paint it? It will mock me some day—mock me horribly!

BASIL: (bitterly) Henry, this is your doing.

HENRY: (shrugging his shoulders) It is the real Dorian Gray—that is all.

BASIL: It is not.

HENRY: If it is not, what have I to do with it?

BASIL: Henry, I can't quarrel with my two best friends at once, but between you both you have made me hate the finest piece of work I have ever done, and I will destroy it. What is it but canvas and colour? I will not let it come across our three lives and mar them.

DORIAN: Don't, Basil, don't destroy it! It would be murder!

BASIL: (coldly) I am glad you appreciate my work at last, Dorian. I never thought you would.

DORIAN: Appreciate it? I am in love with it, Basil. It is part of myself. I feel that.

BASIL: Well, as soon as you are dry, you shall be varnished, and framed, and sent home. Then you can do what you like with yourself.

HENRY: I wish you chaps would not squabble over the picture. You had much better let me have it, Basil. This silly boy doesn't really want it, and I really do.

DORIAN: (with anger) If you let any one have it but me, Basil, I shall never forgive you! And, I don't allow people to call me a silly boy.

HENRY: You know you have been a little silly, Mr. Gray, and that you don't really object to being reminded that you are extremely young. To change the subject, let us go to the theatre tonight. There is sure to be something on, somewhere. I have promised to dine at White's, but it is only with an old friend, so I can send him a wire to say that I am ill, or that I am prevented from coming in consequence of a subsequent engagement. I think that would be a rather nice excuse: it would have all the surprise of candour.

BASIL: (muttering) It is such a bore putting on one's dress clothes. And, when one has them on, they are so horrid.

HENRY: Yes, the costume of the nineteenth-century is detestable. It is so somber, so depressing. Sin is the only real colour-element left in modern life.

BASIL: You really must not say things like that before Dorian, Henry.

HENRY: Before which Dorian? The one sitting here, or the one in the picture?

BASIL: Before either.

DORIAN: I should like to come to the theatre with you, Lord Henry.

HENRY: (invitingly) Then you shall come; and you will come too, Basil, won't you?

BASIL: (firmly) I can't really. I would sooner not. I have a lot of work to do.

HENRY: Well, then, you and I will go alone, Mr. Gray.

DORIAN: I should like that awfully.

BASIL: (sadly) Then I shall stay with the real Dorian.

DORIAN: Is it the real Dorian? Am I really like that?

BASIL: Yes, you are just like that.

DORIAN: How wonderful, Basil!

BASIL: (sighing) At least you are like it in appearance. But it will never alter. That is something.

HENRY: What a fuss people make about fidelity.

BASIL: Don't go to the theatre tonight, Dorian. Stop and dine with me.

DORIAN: I can't, Basil.

BASIL: Why?

DORIAN: Because I have promised Lord Henry Wotton to go with him.

BASIL: He won't like you the better for keeping your promises. He always breaks his own. I beg you not to go.

DORIAN: (laughing and shaking his head)

BASIL: (with deep emotion) I entreat you.

DORIAN: (hesitating and looking over at Lord Henry) I must go, Basil.

BASIL: Very well. It is rather late, and, as you have to dress, you had better lose no time. Good-bye, Henry. Good-bye, Dorian. Come and see me soon. Come tomorrow.

DORIAN: Certainly.

BASIL: You won't forget?

DORIAN: No, of course not.

BASIL: And ... Henry!

HENRY: Yes, Basil?

BASIL: Remember what I asked you about your influence and our friend?

HENRY: (flippantly) I have forgotten it.

BASIL: (quietly) I trust you.

HENRY: I wish I could trust myself. Good-bye, Basil. It has been a most interesting afternoon.

NARRATOR: As his two friends leave, Basil flings himself down on a sofa, and a look of pain comes into his face. Not only has he failed to keep Dorian from Henry's influence, but also he has realized the power of that influence which could alter a kind friend in one afternoon and create a duplicate personality now living in the picture of Dorian Gray. And, it is the picture of Dorian Gray that will disclose the horror of a soul that has been sold for eternal youth.

SCRIPTING NOTES

1. All references to Lord Henry Wotton have been consistent; the nickname Harry which Basil sometimes used has been replaced.

2. Some of the longer speeches have been shortened and/or omitted.

3. Movement in this scene (e.g., Dorian's movement to and from the model's platform) was not adapted into the lines, but rather omitted entirely.

4. Although the action in the text shifted to the outdoors and then back inside, the lines were adapted to indicate a single setting.

5. Extraneous dialogue (e.g., that concerning the serving of refreshments) was omitted.

Part III
SUGGESTED SCRIPTS

This section includes recommendations for developing scripts from forty young adult novels that were selected for their literary quality and popular appeal with young people. In addition, these books are easily adapted to readers theatre because of the dramatic nature of specific scenes.

The suggested scripts for each novel contain identification of an appropriate scene, staging ideas, the narrator's opening and closing lines, and recommendations for developing and delivering the presentation. These suggested scripts should be given to young people who have read the works and who have received instruction from the teacher or librarian on the scripting techniques identified in part I to this work. Many basic ideas suggested there have not been repeated in individual scripts.

In order to adhere to the copyright law, the material which young people develop may be used only for study and instructional purposes and for classroom presentation. Those works protected by copyright law cannot be presented in public, sold, or distributed without permission of the copyright owner.

WOLF RIDER
A Tale of Terror
Avi

A suggested script for Avi's *Wolf Rider* is the scene early in part II when Andy is called into the school counselor's office.

SUGGESTED STAGING

The narrator stands at a lectern. Andy sits on a straight chair; the counselor sits in a chair at a desk.

	Andy	Counselor
	X	X
Narrator		
X		

NARRATOR'S OPENING LINES

We have chosen to read the scene from *Wolf Rider* by Avi in which Andy has been called to the school counselor's office and can't imagine why. The characters are Andy, a fifteen-year-old Madison High School student, read by _____, and Mrs. Baskin, the school counselor, read by _____. I, _____, am the narrator.

Andy receives a weird phone call one evening from someone named Zeke, who says he has just killed Nina Klemmer, a college student. The police and Andy's father feel it is a prank call. Much to the consternation of the police, Andy tries to locate Nina and warn her. Mrs. Baskin's request for Andy to see her is in response to the police officer's call. As the scene opens, Andy is seated in the counselor's office.

SUGGESTIONS FOR SCRIPTING

1. Be sure to give the reader clues to Andy's quickly changing mood—puzzlement, exasperation, sadness, etc.

2. Following Mrs. Baskin's request for him to tell her about the phone call, write Andy's response in which he *briefly* explains the telephone call and his attempts to get the police to warn Nina. As Andy talks, have Mrs. Baskin nod encouragement at first, then become very serious as she feels she has figured out the cause of Andy's problem.

3. Andy's bodily movement changes as he first sits casually, then bolts upright, then slumps down as he thinks of his mother's death. After his rigid position shows his disgust, he sits forward in his chair, trying to understand Mrs. Baskin's implications. These movements help the audience see the emotion Andy feels.

4. End the scene after Andy asks if he has the choice of not coming back to see the counselor and she tells him he does not.

NARRATOR'S CLOSING LINES

In his efforts to prove the "wolf" real, Andy continues his attempt to warn the disbelieving Nina. The threat of danger mounts until it engulfs Andy as well.

TRACKS

Clayton Bess

A suggested script from *Tracks* by Clayton Bess is taken from chapter 2 when Blue follows Monroe into a boxcar of a moving freight train.

SUGGESTED STAGING

The narrator stands at a lectern. Blue, Monroe, Earl, and Bosco Pete are sitting on the floor.

	Monroe		Bosco Pete
	X		X
Blue		Earl	
X		X	
Narrator			
X			

NARRATOR'S OPENING LINES

We will share a scene from *Tracks* by Clayton Bess. The characters are Monroe, a teenager from Atoka, Oklahoma, who is hopping freight trains to California during the Great Depression in pursuit of two girls, read by _____; Monroe's eleven-year-old brother Blue, who follows him without permission, read by _____; and two hoboes who share the boxcar: Earl, read by _____; and Bosco Pete, read by _____. I, _____, am the narrator.

In this scene Blue has almost been killed as he tries to follow Monroe into the boxcar of a moving train. In his fright he messes his jeans and must sit downwind because he smells so bad. Monroe introduces Blue to the two hoboes in the boxcar with him.

SUGGESTIONS FOR SCRIPTING

1. Begin with Monroe's introduction of Earl and Bosco Pete to Blue.

2. Be sure Monroe's reader is given clues to Monroe's anger that Blue has followed him and to his determination that Blue will go back.

3. After Blue tells Monroe that he could at least write goodbye and sign his name to his mother's note, give the narrator a speech such as the following: The train ride is lonesome for Blue. Monroe says no more to him for the rest of the trip. It is growing dark as the train pulls into McAlester and slows down.

4. Let the readers stay seated as they make farewell speeches to each other. Add Earl's name to Bosco Pete's speech, and have Earl call Monroe by name for his final speech so the audience will know who is addressed.

5. End the scene with Monroe's telling Blue that they are getting off.

NARRATOR'S CLOSING LINES

Blue convinces Monroe to let him go on to California. Almost unbelievable dangers await them, and the bitter picture of the Depression will never be forgotten by those who read *Tracks* by Clayton Bess.

ALL THE DAYS WERE SUMMER
Jack Bickham

This suggested script is taken from chapter 7 beginning with one of Danny's conversations with Rudi.

SUGGESTED STAGING
The narrator stands at a lectern. Danny and Rudi sit on stools.

	Danny	Rudi
	X	X
Narrator		
X		

NARRATOR'S OPENING LINES
The scene that we have chosen to share is from Jack Bickham's novel *All the Days Were Summer*. The characters in this scene are Danny Davidson, a lonely and vulnerable twelve-year-old, read by _____, and Rudi, a German POW, read by _____. I, _____, am the narrator.

Danny and Rudi have more in common than Rudi's being a German POW in an Ohio prison camp where Danny's father works as a guard during World War II. Danny has given his heart to a blind German shepherd puppy named Skipper, and Rudi, a veterinarian, knows how to train and care for the handicapped puppy. The hint of a friendship develops between the two as Danny takes advantage of opportunities to visit with Rudi and to seek his advice.

SUGGESTIONS FOR SCRIPTING
1. Begin the scene with Rudi's asking whether Skipper recognizes Danny's voice.

2. Cut the script with Rudi's comment that more discipline is required for a dog or a person who has troubles. Skip the next paragraphs and continue the script with Danny's statement that Rudi must know everything about dogs. Do not explain this adaptation to the audience.

3. Include instructions for the readers to communicate emotions to the audience. Danny is untrusting, but driven by the need for information; Rudi is sad.

4. Before Danny's question about what it was like in Africa, insert the following lines for the narrator: At this time whistles sound, and the guards order the prisoners back to work. As Rudi starts to limp away, Danny calls after him.

5. End the scene with Rudi's description of Germany.

6. This story is told in first person. Adapt the narrator's lines to the third person.

NARRATOR'S CLOSING LINES
With the guards snapping, Rudi limps away. Danny watches him, wondering how this German who loves home, children, and singing can be reconciled with the Germans who are known for the blitzkrieg, storm troopers, and Hitler. Eventually Danny works his way through a confusion of values and emotions, and a warm and genuine friendship develops between him and Rudi. The blind puppy grows and matures and, through firm and wise training, gives Danny love and devotion that exceeds any he has ever known.

TIGER EYES
Judy Blume

The following scene from Judy Blume's *Tiger Eyes* is taken from chapter 2 when Lenaya comes to see Davey.

SUGGESTED STAGING

The narrator stands at a lectern. Davey and Lenaya sit on chairs.

Davey   Lenaya

X   X

Narrator

X

NARRATOR'S OPENING LINES

The characters are fifteen-year-old Davey, who cannot cope with her father's murder, read by _____; and Lenaya, a friend who has come over to see her, read by _____. I, _____, am the narrator.

As the scene opens, Lenaya is sitting on the edge of Davey's bed.

SUGGESTIONS FOR SCRIPTING

1. Start with Lenaya's asking Davey how she is.

2. This is a very emotional time, and Davey struggles to keep from crying. Give Davey's reader directions to nod rather than talk.

3. Later, Davey reads from the paper, desperately trying to control her voice.

4. After Davey reads the lines about contributions to the heart fund, the narrator may say: Davey's Aunt Betsy comes to the door and offers to bring in a tray of food for lunch. Davey doesn't want to eat, but her aunt insists and leaves.

5. Continue with Davey's explanation that Aunt Betsy's real name is Elizabeth.

6. End the scene as Lenaya says she has been talking to Uncle Walter.

NARRATOR'S CLOSING LINES

Davey's mother is near collapse, so Davey, her mother, and her little brother Jason go to live with Uncle Walter and Aunt Betsy. Davey meets a young man in Los Alamos canyon, and he helps her face her grief.

SOMETHING WICKED THIS WAY COMES

Ray Bradbury

The following scene from Ray Bradbury's *Something Wicked This Way Comes* is taken from chapter 28 where Will Halloway and his dad linger late in the night to talk man to boy-becoming-man.

SUGGESTED STAGING

The narrator stands at a lectern. Will and Charles sit on stools.

Will Halloway
X

Charles Halloway
X

Narrator
X

NARRATOR'S OPENING LINES

The scene that we have chosen to share is from Ray Bradbury's *Something Wicked This Way Comes*. The characters are Will Halloway, a thirteen-year-old boy, read by _____, and Will's father Charles Halloway, a fifty-four-year-old janitor, read by _____. I, _____, am the narrator.

Will has discovered the wicked thing that has come to Green Town; and, deciding that safety exists only in ignorance, he determines that he must not put his dad in jeopardy by confiding what he has seen. However, as Will wrestles alone with his fear, he seeks his dad's support and advice. On this evening they talk late into the night.

SUGGESTIONS FOR SCRIPTING

1. Begin with Will's asking whether he is a good person.

2. Condense the three consecutive long paragraphs of the dad's dialogue.

3. Adapt Will's thought that the carnival is both life and death into lines for the narrator.

4. End the script with the dad's promising that he does trust Will.

NARRATOR'S CLOSING LINES

The two decide that it is time to go inside, and Will invites his dad to join him in climbing through a second-floor window into the house. At first his dad declines; then he accepts. Other challenges will come to that middle-aged father and the boy-becoming-man. They will both need extraordinary strength and energy to meet something wicked that this way comes.

THE MOVES MAKE THE MAN
Bruce Brooks

This script is taken from chapter 18 where Jerome Foxworthy and Bix Rivers are taught to make mock-apple pie.

SUGGESTED STAGING

This novel is a first-person account by Jerome Foxworthy; because that point of view is maintained in this script, Jerome is both a character and the narrator. All characters sit in chairs.

NARRATOR'S OPENING LINES

Jerome: (businesslike) The script that we have chosen to share is from *The Moves Make the Man* by Bruce Brooks. The characters in this scene are Bix, one fine baseball player, read by _____; Miss Pimton, a not-so-sensible home economics teacher, read by _____; three of the girls in the class, read by _____, _____, and _____; and Jerome Foxworthy, the only black student in the school, read by me, _____.

(with amused disgust) This home ec class has been some display of nonsense. I am enrolled in it because my mother is in the hospital, and I am responsible for the cooking at home. What have I learned so far? I have learned how to put on an apron and how to make patties from shredded newspapers. And the rest of the class? The girls think everything is cute and exciting, and Bix is a limp fish, sitting all hunkered down in his desk. And what are we doing today? We're making mock-apple pie — that's right, mock-apple pie.

SUGGESTIONS FOR SCRIPTING

1. Continue the scene by creating dialogue for Miss Pimton so that she can provide some explanation for the assignment and give the recipe.

2. Next direct Jerome to read the first two paragraphs of chapter 18.

3. From the third paragraph of the chapter create appropriate dialogue for the girls and Miss Pimton.

4. Until this point Jerome, as narrator, has kept his attention on the audience. However, beginning with his comment about fooling people with crackers and water, he is a full participant in the scene. Therefore, his position should shift so that he faces the audience and yet interacts with the other characters through body language. Provide adequate instructions for Jerome's reader to interpret both roles.

5. Do not assign Jerome to read descriptions of the other characters, but rather create directions for their appropriate body language.

6. Omit movements, such as Bix's walking.

7. With Jerome squarely facing the audience, end the scene with his reading the last two paragraphs and then the narrator's closing lines.

8. Use a consistent form of Bix's name.

NARRATOR'S CLOSING LINES

What I didn't know then was how seriously Bix took anything that is fake or mock. Bix has emotional problems, and the slender thread that keeps him in the real world cannot tolerate a lie, a false compliment, a fake move on the basketball court, or a mock-apple pie. Only when I learn the terrible price Bix has paid for "truth" do I begin to understand his inability to compromise.

LEROY AND THE OLD MAN

W. E. Butterworth

The following suggested script is from the opening of W. E. Butterworth's novel *LeRoy and the Old Man*. In this scene the police question LeRoy about his having witnessed an assault and robbery.

SUGGESTED STAGING
The narrator stands at a lectern. LeRoy and the policemen stand.

LeRoy   The Junkie

X   X

Policeman

X

Narrator

X

NARRATOR'S OPENING LINES
The scene that we have chosen to share is from the opening of W. E. Butterworth's novel *LeRoy and the Old Man*. The characters in this scene are LeRoy, a young black man, read by _____; the junkie, a plainclothes cop, read by _____; a uniformed cop, read by _____. I, _____, am the narrator.

LeRoy has just returned from work to his building in a Chicago housing project. The junkie and the uniformed cop are waiting in the hall for him.

SUGGESTIONS FOR SCRIPTING
1. The scene begins as the junkie asks LeRoy whether he has a minute.

2. LeRoy is lying, and his voice and actions must give clues that fear is holding back the truth.

3. The fact that the cops rough up LeRoy should not be acted out but rather should be incorporated into LeRoy's dialogue, for example as he protests their actions. Create those lines.

4. The cop's tough and aggressive behavior should be communicated through directions given to the readers.

5. The scene should end with the uniformed cop's telling LeRoy to get out of his sight.

NARRATOR'S CLOSING LINES
LeRoy takes the elevator to the sixth floor where he finds the attackers are waiting for him. They threaten him with a switchblade and later return to vandalize his mother's apartment. When his mother realizes there is no safety for LeRoy in Chicago, she persuades him to go to Christian, Mississippi, where the Old Man, his paternal grandfather, lives. The Old Man is a demanding and resourceful commercial fisherman, and he offers LeRoy a different way of life.

THE TAMARACK TREE
Patricia Clapp

The following suggested adaptation of Patricia Clapp's *The Tamarack Tree* is taken from the chapter "April 1861."

SUGGESTED STAGING
The narrator stands at a lectern. Jeff and Rosemary sit in armchairs.

Jeff   Rosemary

X   X

Narrator

X

NARRATOR'S OPENING LINES
We will share a selection from *The Tamarack Tree* by Patricia Clapp. In this scene, a sixteen-year-old British girl, Rosemary, is read by _____. Her brother Derek brought her to Vicksburg, Mississippi, three years ago after their mother's death. Jeff Howard, a Harvard University student visiting Uncle Will's family during the holidays, is read by _____. I, _____, am the narrator.

The year is 1861, and Jeff has just shown Rosemary an article in the latest issue of the newspaper.

SUGGESTIONS FOR SCRIPTING
1. Begin with Jeff's questioning Rosemary about whether she has read the Beauregard story.

2. Have Jeff and Rosemary remain seated. Their impatience, evidenced in the book by walking around the room, can be shown by voice and bodily tension.

3. Give the readers directions to indicate changes in emotion — softly, angrily, sincerely, tearfully, etc.

4. Let the scene end with Rosemary's emotional speech that Jeff can tell the people he kills how sorry he is. She runs from the room and Jeff goes off slowly in the opposite direction with his head down.

NARRATOR'S CLOSING LINES
The next two years bring many physical and emotional hardships for Rosemary, ending with the forty-seven-day siege of Vicksburg in 1863. Rosemary finally finds hope in the silly teasing poem about the tamarack tree to which Jeff has added a verse showing that he will protect her.

WEEKEND SISTERS
Hila Colman

The following suggested scene from *Weekend Sisters* by Hila Colman is taken from chapter 1 when fourteen-year-old Amanda's mother tells her that Amanda's divorced father plans to marry again.

SUGGESTED STAGING
The narrator stands at a lectern. Amanda and her mother sit on chairs.

	Amanda	Her Mother
	X	X
Narrator		
X		

NARRATOR'S OPENING LINES
We will share a scene from *Weekend Sisters* by Hila Colman. The characters are fourteen-year-old Amanda, read by _____, and her divorced mother, read by _____. I, _____, am the narrator.

After her parents' divorce Amanda has been living with her mother during the week and with her father on weekends. Tonight Amanda and her mother are sitting in the living room. From her mother's determined expression, Amanda is sure bad news is forthcoming.

SUGGESTIONS FOR SCRIPTING
1. Begin with her mother's saying that she has something she must tell Amanda.

2. Be sure to give the reader directions for Amanda's shocked expression, loud voice, anger, and dismay.

3. Close with the mother's saying it is time to have supper as she is hungry.

NARRATOR'S CLOSING LINES
Amanda's problems are just beginning. Fern steals for fun and shows no concern for Amanda's feelings. Amanda fears she is losing her father's love but finally realizes she is just lending him for a time.

PRAIRIE SONGS
Pam Conrad

The following suggested adaptation of a scene from Pam Conrad's *Prairie Songs* is taken from chapter 4 when the newly arrived New York doctor and his wife are having dinner with the Downings, a Nebraska pioneer family.

SUGGESTED STAGING
The narrator stands at a lectern. The rest sit on a variety of unmatched chairs.

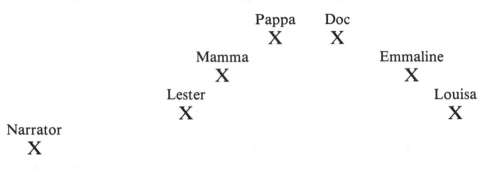

```
                    Pappa    Doc
                     X        X
              Mamma                  Emmaline
                X                       X
         Lester                             Louisa
           X                                  X
    Narrator
      X
```

NARRATOR'S OPENING LINES
We will share a scene from *Prairie Songs* by Pam Conrad. The characters for the selection we have chosen are young Doc Berryman, read by _____; Emmaline Berryman, a fragile, frightened woman, read by _____; hardy Mr. Downing (Pappa), read by _____; his wife Clara (Mamma), read by _____; and the Downing's two children: outgoing Louisa, read by _____, and Lester, her quiet little brother, read by _____. I, _____, am the narrator.

Dr. Berryman and his wife have recently arrived in frontier Nebraska from New York. Mrs. Berryman is shocked at the lonely prairie, the sod house with a dirt floor, and the need to collect cow chips to burn for fuel. They are now seated at the dinner table of the Downings, a family living three miles from them.

SUGGESTIONS FOR SCRIPTING
1. Begin having Mrs. Berryman say that the dinner smells wonderful and admit that she is not a good cook.

2. Do not be concerned about eating. Let the conversation and the display of emotion be the important aspect.

3. After Mrs. Downing assures Mrs. Berryman that she can't wait to see the cradle, insert the following narrator speech: Mrs. Downing suggests that they move their chairs outside and eat their applesauce made from apples imported from Philadelphia.

4. Then have Mrs. Downing remark that it is peaceful.

5. Be sure to note the family's surprise at Dr. Berryman's sharp words to his wife.

6. End with Mrs. Downing's invitation for Mrs. Berryman to see her vegetable garden.

NARRATOR'S CLOSING LINES
Louisa's life is changed as the frail Mrs. Berryman teaches the children to read. Then the lonely prairie with all its problems prompts a tragedy.

I AM THE CHEESE

Robert Cormier

The following scene from *I Am the Cheese* by Robert Cormier is taken from Tape 0Z K 001 when Adam first meets the interrogator.

SUGGESTED STAGING

The narrator stands at a lectern. Adam sits in a chair. The interrogator sits in a chair after his first speech.

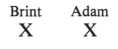

Brint   Adam

X   X

Narrator

X

NARRATOR'S OPENING LINES

We will share a scene from Robert Cormier's *I Am the Cheese*. The characters are Adam Farmer, who is trying to recall the events of a tragedy in his life, read by _____; and Brint, the man who is trying to help Adam remember, read by _____. I, _____, am the narrator.

SUGGESTIONS FOR SCRIPTING

1. Begin the scene with Brint's introducing himself and explaining that they will be spending time together.

2. Be sure the directions for the tone and bodily action of Adam evidence his nervousness, bewilderment, and final concern about whether he should reveal to Brint the clues he remembers.

3. Briefly summarize what Adam tells about that night as follows: Usually when I was lying in bed I could hear my parents' voices, soft and murmuring. However, that night they spoke in loud whispers, and the tone of their voices was harsher. Once I heard my mother try to quiet my father because they might awaken me.

4. End the scene after Adam says that he does not know why he is uncertain.

NARRATOR'S CLOSING LINES

But Adam Farmer did know. He didn't feel entirely comfortable with this stranger and he wasn't sure whether he should tell him about the clues. Thus begins a story of suspense and political intrigue that makes Adam Farmer wonder—in the words of the old song "Farmer in the Dell ... Farmer in the Dell ... The cheese stands alone"—whether he is the cheese.

MAY I CROSS YOUR GOLDEN RIVER?

Paige Dixon

A suggested script for Paige Dixon's *May I Cross Your Golden River?* is taken from the scene in chapter 6 where Jordan and his brother meet with the doctor who has diagnosed Jordan's illness.

SUGGESTED STAGING
The narrator stands at a lectern. Alex and Jordan sit on chairs. The doctor sits on a stool.

Jordan
X   The Doctor
                  X
Alex
X
Narrator
X

NARRATOR'S OPENING LINES
The script we are reading is one that has been adapted from Paige Dixon's *May I Cross Your Golden River?* The characters are Jordan Phillips, who has been undergoing diagnostic tests at Mayo Clinic, read by _____; Jordan's older brother, Alex, who has accompanied him, read by _____; and the doctor who is in charge of Jordan's case, read by _____. I, _____, am the narrator.

Jordan and Alex have come to the Mayo Clinic in Rochester, Minnesota, because the family doctor in Boulder, Colorado, cannot explain Jordan's aches and loss of muscle control. After several days of medical tests, both brothers have been asked to meet with the doctor.

SUGGESTIONS FOR SCRIPTING
1. To communicate emotion, adapt most of the author's descriptions of the participants' behavior into directions for the readers. Examples of those directions include "looking quickly at Alex," "interrupting," "hesitating," "leaning forward tensely," "shaking his head 'no'," "extending his hand," and "turning away."

2. Jordan's reference to the Supreme Court's not having to wait for him requires re-writing so the audience understands that one of Jordan's goals has been to become an attorney.

3. End the scene with only the two brothers remaining in place after the doctor has left quickly. In the last line of the scene Alex suggests that they go. Exhausted, Jordan slumps quietly in his chair.

NARRATOR'S CLOSING LINES
Thus begins one of the many journeys that Jordan and his family must make over the next months. Jordan first experiences anger, bitterness, humiliation, and alienation. He finally sees that meaning in life comes through love, compassion, and brotherhood.

The title, *May I Cross Your Golden River?*, is taken from a children's rhyme that is repeated during a game of tag: "Crocodile, crocodile, may I cross your golden river in your little golden boat?" When Jordan watches the children shouting the rhyme at play, he thinks of his namesake—his sister's soon-to-be-born baby—and the reader knows that Jordan will make a safe and courageous passage over his last river.

I KNOW WHAT YOU DID LAST SUMMER

Lois Duncan

The following scene from *I Know What You Did Last Summer* by Lois Duncan is taken from chapter 3 when Ray stops to see Helen.

SUGGESTED STAGING

The narrator stands at a lectern. Helen and Ray sit on chairs.

                    Helen   Ray
                     X   X

Narrator
  X

NARRATOR'S OPENING LINES

We will share a scene from Lois Duncan's *I Know What You Did Last Summer*. The characters are Ray, who dated Helen last summer, read by _____, and Helen, who spent her senior year in high school studying and trying to forget last summer, read by _____. I, _____, am the narrator.

Ray has just come back from California. Although he and Helen have not kept in touch, he still cares for her and stops to see her.

SUGGESTIONS FOR SCRIPTING

1. Begin the scene when Ray tells Helen he has been thinking about her and wants to see how she is.

2. Let Helen just hand Ray the letter while they both still sit. Have him read the message aloud and then look stunned.

3. Be sure to give clues to the reader for changes in voice — surprise, indifference, sadness, despair, etc.

4. End the scene just before the doorbell rings by having Helen say that Barry will never agree to dissolve the pact.

NARRATOR'S CLOSING LINES

Release from the pact is the only way these two friends can reveal what happened last summer. They can never erase it or undo it, but facing it will be the first step in going on with their lives.

WILDERNESS PERIL
Thomas J. Dygard

A suggested script for *Wilderness Peril* by Thomas J. Dygard begins as Todd and Mike, driving to the Boundary Waters Canoe Area, hear the news about the hijacker.

SUGGESTED STAGING

The narrator stands at a lectern; Mike and Todd sit on chairs.

Mike   Todd

X   X

Narrator

X

NARRATOR'S OPENING LINES

We will read a portion of the first chapter of *Wilderness Peril* by Thomas J. Dygard. The characters are Mike, headed for college on a football scholarship, read by _____; and Todd, a close friend whose athletic interests are canoeing and camping, read by _____. I, _____, am the narrator.

In this scene the two boys are driving toward the Boundary Waters Canoe Area to start a wilderness journey. A radio announcement tells them a hijacker of a Global Airways jet is demanding $750,000 ransom.

SUGGESTIONS FOR SCRIPTING

1. Begin the scene with Mike's comment that three-quarters of a million dollars is a lot of money.

2. After Todd refuses a soda let the narrator say: As Todd gets a soda from the ice chest, the news update announces that Global Airways has agreed to the cash ransom and other demands of the hijacker.

3. Todd is impressed as he comments that the payoff is a lot of money.

4. End with the boys laughing over the idea of lots and lots of money.

NARRATOR'S CLOSING LINES

The boys laugh now, but before their leisurely trip is over, the hijacker's cash ransom becomes *their* nightmare.

FOOTSTEPS

Leon Garfield

The following suggested scene from Leon Garfield's *Footsteps* is taken from the beginning of chapter 2 when William goes to his father's room.

SUGGESTED STAGING

The narrator stands at a lectern. William's father sits in an armchair, and William stands until he is told to sit.

William   William's Father

X   X

Narrator

X

NARRATOR'S OPENING LINES

We shall read a scene from *Footsteps* by Leon Garfield. The characters are William Jones, the son of a wealthy Englishman, read by _____, and William's father, now retired and very ill, read by _____. I, _____, am the narrator.

The setting is a fine old house in Hartford, England, just outside London. William's father's room is just below his, and every night William hears his father pacing the floor after everyone is asleep. One night the footsteps cease and, instead of waking up the family and putting up with cruel Uncle Turner, William goes alone to his father's room. He is afraid his father is dead, but finds him standing behind the door dressed to go out. He helps his father to his chair.

SUGGESTIONS FOR SCRIPTING

1. Have William's father ask William if he hears his father's footsteps at night.

2. The description gives exact clues for conversation not given:

   WILLIAM'S FATHER: Did you tell your mother or anyone else?
   WILLIAM: (shaking his head) No.
   WILLIAM'S FATHER: Did you ever hear me before?
   WILLIAM: (nervously) No.
   WILLIAM'S FATHER: I said, did you hear me before?
   WILLIAM: (fearful of his father's anger) Yes, Pa, many times.

3. Continue filling in conversation as needed.

4. After his father tells him to bring the watch, have the narrator say: William brought his father the watch, and he began to fiddle with the back, trying to insert the key.

5. Omit the father's suggested questions about school, but add the father's speech about the mother and sisters and the repeated direction for winding the clock.

6. William is afraid when his father has the attack. Give the father's reader directions for this seizure.

7. Continue the scene, filling in the brief conversation when William offers to get his mother, and his father tells him not to leave him.

8. Be sure that as his father whispers, it is a stage whisper loud enough to be heard by the audience.

9. Let the final speech be firm and loud as his father confesses he is a thief.

NARRATOR'S CLOSING LINES

William leaves his father's room and later that night his father dies. After the funeral, cruel Uncle Turner accuses William of stealing the watch, and in anger, William tells his father's story. No one believes him. That night William is terrified as he hears his dead father's footsteps. He knows he must go to London and try to make amends so his father's ghost can rest. He has no way of knowing the dangers he will face.

MY LIFE IN THE SEVENTH GRADE
Mark Geller

A suggested script for Mark Geller's *My Life in the Seventh Grade* is the algebra class scene when Mr. Levitt, the substitute teacher who cruelly wants to embarrass Marvin, sends him to the blackboard.

SUGGESTED STAGING
The narrator stands at a lectern. Leonard is seated on a student chair. Mr. Levitt sits on a desk chair. Marvin stands.

<pre>
                                        Marvin   Leonard
                                          X   X

                         Mr. Levitt
                             X

            Narrator
               X
</pre>

NARRATOR'S OPENING LINES
We will share an algebra class scene from *My Life in the Seventh Grade* by Mark Geller. Although the classroom is full of students, only three people have active roles. The characters are Marvin Berman, who hates algebra, read by _____; Leonard Bridgeman, the oldest, toughest boy in class, read by _____; and Mr. Levitt, the substitute teacher, read by _____. I, _____, am the narrator.

On a previous day Marvin Berman has been in trouble with Mr. Levitt, the substitute teacher, for reading a magazine in social studies class. Today, Mr. Levitt sees Marvin's grades in algebra while calling roll and sarcastically comments that algebra is certainly not Marvin's long suit. He calls on Marvin to work some problems on the blackboard. Marvin tells Mr. Levitt he doesn't know how, but Mr. Levitt insists. He says everyone else might learn something from Marvin's mistakes or at least find them entertaining. Marvin stands at the blackboard, humiliated and not knowing how to begin.

SUGGESTIONS FOR SCRIPTING
1. Begin the scene as Leonard Bridgeman calls "Yo" to the teacher from the back of the class.

2. Let Marvin show interest in the scene and begin to listen intently as Leonard calls Marvin his man.

3. Be sure to give directions for Mr. Levitt's nervousness, increased anger, and raised voice.

4. Let Marvin look gratefully at Leonard when he queries the teacher about why he's giving Marvin a hard time.

5. Leonard stands and sits as directed, but should do so slowly.

6. Near the end of the scene when Mr. Levitt asks Marvin if he can do the problems, let Marvin shake his head and answer that he can't.

7. Break up Mr. Levitt's last speech of the scene. When Mr. Levitt tells him to go to his seat, let Marvin ask, "Go to my seat?"

8. The scene closes just before Marvin walks to his seat.

NARRATOR'S CLOSING LINES
Marvin no longer feels humiliated, and a strange friendship with Leonard is cemented which benefits them both.

LORD OF THE FLIES
William Golding

This script is taken from chapter 5 when the assembled boys discuss the possibility of the reported beast being a ghost.

SUGGESTED STAGING
The narrator stands at a lectern. The boys sit on the floor.

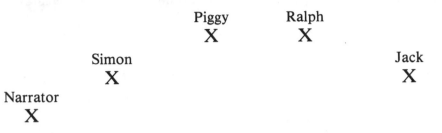

NARRATOR'S OPENING LINES

We are sharing a scene from William Golding's *Lord of the Flies*. The characters in this scene are Jack, the group's aggressive hunter, read by _____; intelligent, but frequently taunted Piggy, read by _____; Ralph, the elected leader, read by _____; and Simon, quietest of the four, read by _____. I, _____, am the narrator.

This group of English schoolboys, shipwreck survivors, are stranded on a coral island. In their attempt to establish order, they agree that in group meetings the speaker is the one who holds the conch shell. At this point the group has assembled in order to deal with several problems, including that during a boar hunt the signal fire has gone out and the young ones have reported seeing a mysterious beast. It has been suggested that perhaps the beast is a ghost.

SUGGESTIONS FOR SCRIPTING

1. Begin the scene as Piggy indignantly states that he does not believe in ghosts.

2. After Jack shouts that he has the conch shell, use the following narrator's lines: There was a quick fight. Amid shouts and the exchange of blows, Ralph seizes the conch shell and sits down.

3. Continue with Ralph's lines, combining his next two speeches. Provide adequate instructions for the variation of emotion in Ralph's speeches—at first breathless, later flat, and always struggling for agreement.

4. Omit all movement except those small gestures that communicate mood and emotion.

5. Omit the line given by the anonymous voice.

6. Except for the four speaking characters and the narrator, omit references to any others present.

7. Omit all descriptions by the author except those that have been adapted below into the narrator's dialogue.

8. After Ralph's comment that he sees, use the following narrator's lines: Piggy leaps up and grabs the conch shell.

9. After Jack calls Piggy a *slug*, use the following narrator's lines: Furiously Jack turns on Piggy, and there is another struggle.

10. After Jack shouts that they will hunt the beast down, instruct his reader to leave the stage.

11. End the scene with Piggy's wish that grown-ups would send a message.

NARRATOR'S CLOSING LINES

However, there is no saving message for this tragic group of schoolboys, and they revert more deeply to anarchy and savagery. If there *is* a message it is for the novel's readers: How are we as individuals and societies different from this stranded group of schoolboys?

SUMMER OF MY GERMAN SOLDIER
Betty Greene

The following scene is from chapter 3 of Betty Greene's *Summer of My German Soldier* when Patty waits on Reiker in her father's store.

SUGGESTED STAGING

The narrator stands at a lectern. Reiker, Patty, and Sister Parker are seated on stools.

Patty
X

Reiker   Sister Parker
X   X

Narrator
X

NARRATOR'S OPENING LINES

We shall share a scene from Betty Greene's *Summer of My German Soldier*. The characters are Patty Bergen, a Jewish girl who is desperate for friendship and parental affection, read by _____; Anton Reiker, a German prisoner of war, read by _____; and Sister Parker, who works in Patty's father's store, read by _____. I, _____, am the narrator.

The scene is Jenkinsville, Arkansas, during World War II. Reiker and some other prisoners of war have come into the Bergen store where Patty is working. They need hats to work in the cotton fields. Reiker wanders away from the others and Patty goes over to help him.

SUGGESTIONS FOR SCRIPTING

1. Begin by having Patty ask Anton Reiker if she can help him.

2. Let the readers' voices and smiles indicate how quickly they become friends.

3. End this part of the scene when Anton tells Patty that, when they meet again, she can tell him her conclusions.

4. Then use a narrator to introduce the next part of the scene thus: The guard calls the prisoners to get ready to leave, so Anton tells Patty good-bye. While Anton and Patty were talking, across the store Sister Parker is listening and watching. Later that day Patty approaches her to talk about the prisoners.

5. Begin with Patty's saying it is interesting to have the Germans come in.

6. End with Patty's telling Sister Parker that all she has to do is ask.

NARRATOR'S CLOSING LINES

Patty and Anton become friends, but their story is a tragic one.

ORDINARY PEOPLE
Judith Guest

The following suggested script from chapter 5 of Judith Guest's *Ordinary People* is adapted from Conrad's first visit with his psychiatrist, Dr. Berger.

SUGGESTED STAGING

The narrator stands at a lectern. Conrad sits in a chair; Dr. Berger sits at his desk.

Conrad Jarrett   Dr. Berger

X   X

Narrator

X

NARRATOR'S OPENING LINES

This readers script has been adapted from Judith Guest's *Ordinary People*. The characters in this scene are Conrad Jarrett, a disturbed high school student, read by _____, and Conrad's psychiatrist, Dr. Berger, read by _____. I, _____, am the narrator.

Conrad, having spent the last year in a mental hospital, has returned home with the understanding that he must continue regular appointments with a psychiatrist. He does not trust psychiatrists; and when he enters the office of his new doctor, he is suspicious that a put-on has been staged. The office is in a shambles. Furniture is overturned and books have been tossed on the floor. Dr. Berger, hunched at his desk in the midst of the chaos, looks up and sees Conrad.

SUGGESTIONS FOR SCRIPTING

1. Begin the scene by having the doctor ask Conrad to wait.

2. Provide instructions for reading so that the doctor's open and good-natured approach is evident.

3. Conrad's emotions vary from cold politeness to near panic and finally laughter; provide clues to help the reader interpret his lines appropriately.

4. Incorporate into the doctor's lines information about the spilled files and other facts that are necessary to understand his lines.

5. Adapt descriptions of characters' motions into directions for gestures—for example, the doctor raises his arm palm up to indicate perplexity.

6. End the script with the doctor's statement that he is the doctor and Conrad is the patient.

7. Omit the doctor's movement as he sorts through items in the disorganized office.

NARRATOR'S CLOSING LINES

Conrad leaves the doctor's thankful that the first and the most difficult session is over and that with the doctor nothing is hidden. Physically Conrad has returned home from the hospital, but it will take many months before he can mentally and spiritually return home. Conrad depends on the open honesty of Dr. Berger; and when he finally thanks the doctor and tells him good-bye, he rates him a nine.

THE DISAPPEARANCE
Rosa Guy

This suggested scene is taken from chapter 12 where the Aimsleys and Dora Lee are alone in the kitchen after the police have taken Imamu away.

SUGGESTED STAGING
The narrator stands at a lectern. Peter, Ann, Gail Aimsley, and Dora Lee sit on stools.

```
                            Peter     Ann
                  Gail        X        X        Dora Lee
                   X                                 X
         Narrator
            X
```

NARRATOR'S OPENING LINES
The scene that we are sharing is from *The Disappearance* by Rosa Guy. Three of the characters in this scene are from the Aimsley family. Gail Aimsley is a sensitive young adult, read by _____; Peter Aimsley is Gail's father, read by _____; and Ann Aimsley is Gail's mother, read by _____. Dora Lee is an old family friend, read by _____. I, _____, am the narrator.

This scene occurs at a crisis point for the Aimsley family. Perk, the adored younger daughter, is missing. The police have just left, taking with them the main character, Imamu Jones, as a suspect. A major clue implicating Imamu is the assumption that blood found near the sink is that of Perk, the missing child. However, the blood stains are Imamu's, and they were left there after he accidentally broke one of Ann Aimsley's crystal glasses. The mother Ann feels that Imamu is guilty and blames herself because she brought Imamu into their middle-class household to give him an opportunity to succeed away from dirty Harlem streets.

SCRIPTING NOTES
1. Begin the scene with Ann Aimsley's sobbing that the disappearance is her fault.

2. Each reader will need clear instructions about the emotions that are portrayed. Dora Lee is confused; Ann is self-pitying; Peter is confused and yet desperately trying to console his wife; Gail is embarrassed and angry. Instruct each reader separately before the first lines are read.

3. Continue to convey the emotion of the scene by providing instructions for each reader. Adapt clues from the text (e.g., shouted, whimpering, and screamed).

4. In order to communicate the action of Gail in search of the broken glass and counting the pieces of crystal, create appropriate lines to be read by the narrator.

5. End the scene with Dora Lee's offer that Imamu can stay with her. Instruct the Aimsleys to stare at her.

NARRATOR'S CLOSING LINES
Betrayed by a hysterical family that only the day before had offered friendship, Imamu Jones must find the strength within himself not only to prove his innocence but also to find the missing child.

THE SOLITARY
Lynn Hall

The following scene from Lynn Hall's *The Solitary* begins in chapter 4 as Jane and Iva sit by the wood stove in Iva's living room behind the store.

SUGGESTED STAGING

The narrator stands at a lectern. Jane and Iva are sitting on chairs.

Jane   Iva
  X   X

Narrator
  X

NARRATOR'S OPENING LINES

We will share a scene from Lynn Hall's *The Solitary*. The characters are seventeen-year-old Jane Cahill, read by _____, and Iva, read by _____. I, _____, am the narrator.

After living for years with an uncle and aunt who did not want her, Jane Cahill moves back to the dilapidated, sagging house where her mother had killed her father twelve years earlier. She buys some rabbits to breed and tries to make a living. She makes friends with Iva, who owns the country filling station and store. Iva is the only one who feels Jane is not making a mistake by living there alone.

As the scene opens, Jane and Iva are sitting by the wood stove in Iva's cluttered living room behind the store.

SUGGESTIONS FOR SCRIPTING

1. Begin with Jane's speech that Beau and Marian make her feel as though she is making a mistake by living there alone.

2. Many words are used to show the changing moods of Iva and Jane—laughing, thoughtful, pondered, chuckled, snorted, etc. Be sure to convey these directions to the reader.

3. End the scene with the end of the chapter as Iva tells Jane to follow her own instincts and not listen to anyone else.

NARRATOR'S CLOSING LINES

As Jane lay in bed that night, she pondered Iva's closing remark. Her instincts told her to stay where she was, enjoying her aloneness and building a life for herself. Yet was that feeling an instinct—or was it cowardice?

TEX

S. E. Hinton

The following scene from S. E. Hinton's *Tex* is taken from chapter 1 as Tex comes home and finds a depressed Mace sitting in the kitchen.

SUGGESTED STAGING

The narrator stands at a lectern; Tex and Mace sit on chairs.

Tex   Mace
X   X

Narrator
X

NARRATOR'S OPENING LINES

We have chosen to read the scene from S. E. Hinton's *Tex*. The characters are easy-going, fifteen-year-old Tex, read by _____, and his older brother Mace, a responsible high school senior, read by _____. I, _____, am the narrator.

Mace must maintain their ramshackle house, care for Tex, and make ends meet while their irresponsible, rodeo-riding father is away. Tex has few worries, so he is surprised to find a depressed Mace sitting by the kitchen table as he returns home.

SUGGESTIONS FOR SCRIPTING

1. Begin having Tex tell Mace that he spooked him and have Tex ask Mace why he is home. Have Tex seated by the table at that time.

2. There is a great contrast in the personalities of Tex and Mace. Be sure the readers of the script are given clues to Tex's irresponsible attitude and the seriousness and discouragement of Mace.

3. End the scene with Tex's shocked disbelief as Mace tells him he sold the horses for a good price.

NARRATOR'S CLOSING LINES

Tex dashes from the room and finds Negrito is gone. He fights with Mace and goes out determined to find his horse. That is only the beginning of his struggle with the reality of growing up.

CAT, HERSELF

Mollie Hunter

The following scene from *Cat, Herself* by Mollie Hunter begins in chapter 4 as Cat meets Charlie on the riverbank path.

SUGGESTED STAGING

The narrator stands at a lectern. Cat and Charlie are sitting on stools.

Cat   Charlie

X   X

Narrator

X

NARRATOR'S OPENING LINES

We have chosen a scene from *Cat, Herself* by Mollie Hunter. The characters are Catriona McPhie, the daughter of Jim McPhie whose family wanders the Scottish countryside, read by _____; and Charlie Drummond, a young man whose family are also Scottish travellers, read by _____. I, _____, am the narrator.

Cat is worried about Charlie because his drunken dad has cruelly beaten his mother, and Charlie, in anger, vows to kill his father. Today, they meet on a riverbank where Cat is intently watching a group of swans in flight.

SUGGESTIONS FOR SCRIPTING

1. To open the scene have Cat sit facing the narrator, intently watching the swans. Then she turns on her stool in surprise as Charlie calls her name.

2. Note the changes in body language and voice for the reader of the script—grinning, surprise, embarrassment, confusion, scorn, teasing, anger, dismay, etc.

3. Omit the miming of pearl fishing that Charlie does. Let Cat ask to go with him after Charlie says he's going to try it.

4. Let Charlie's voice show his pleading rather than his attempt to grab Cat's arm.

5. End having Cat shout that Charlie should not say things he doesn't mean. Let her run off stage in one direction. Charlie shrugs his shoulders and saunters off in the other direction.

NARRATOR'S CLOSING LINES

Cat is furious that she has wasted her sympathy on Charlie. She is sure she'll never make that mistake again. Cat learns the traveller skills of men from her father and copes with the problems facing a woman wanting to avoid the limiting restrictions placed on traveller women.

ABBY, MY LOVE
Hadley Irwin

The following scene from Hadley Irwin's *Abby, My Love* is taken from chapter 4 when Chip catches up with Abby on the way home from school.

SUGGESTED STAGING
The narrator stands at a lectern. Abby and Chip sit on stools.

Abby   Chip

X   X

Narrator

X

NARRATOR'S OPENING LINES
We shall share a scene from *Abby, My Love* by Hadley Irwin. The characters are Chip, who has loved Abby since she was twelve, read by _____, and Abby, a dentist's daughter who must learn to control her own life, read by _____. I, _____, am the narrator.

Chip and Abby are high school friends, but Abby is hard to understand: one day Abby will be friendly, the next day withdrawn. One Monday Chip follows Abby out of English class.

SUGGESTIONS FOR SCRIPTING
1. Begin the scene with Chip's telling Abby to hold up so he can walk with her.

2. Abby becomes upset at the end of the scene. Direct the reader to express this change in mood.

3. End the scene with Abby's emotional warning that Chip must never laugh at her.

NARRATOR'S CLOSING LINES
As Chip watches Abby run into her house, he wonders what he has said that upset her. Chip will never laugh at Abby; and when she finally tells him the horrible secret that explains her moods, it is Chip who helps her control her own life.

GENTLEHANDS
M. E. Kerr

A suggested script for M. E. Kerr's *Gentlehands* is taken from the last part of chapter 10, beginning with the mother's question of how Buddy got to work.

SUGGESTED STAGING

The narrator stands at a lectern. Buddy and his mother sit on chairs.

Buddy   Mother
X   X

Narrator
X

NARRATOR'S OPENING LINES

We have chosen to read an excerpt from *Gentlehands* by M. E. Kerr. The characters in this scene are Buddy Boyle, a poor boy attempting to impress his wealthy girl friend, read by _____, and Buddy's mother, a policeman's wife estranged from her well-to-do father, read by _____. I, _____, am the narrator.

In this scene Buddy is taking a break from the soda shop where he works, and he finds his mother waiting to see him. They go to a parking lot and sit in her Toyota to talk about the increasingly unpleasant difficulties between Buddy and his father. The problems between Buddy and his father stem from Buddy's relationships with his wealthy girl friend and his maternal grandfather.

SUGGESTIONS FOR SCRIPTING

1. To establish character identity for the audience, have Buddy's mother address him by name as she asks him how he got to work.

2. The script almost writes itself as you eliminate "she demanded," "I said," etc.

3. The emotional impact of the scene increases in intensity. Give directions in parentheses for reading the various individual lines—(e.g., sobbing, quietly, raising his voice, etc.).

4. Substitute names for pronouns as needed to make sure the audience understands the speech.

5. Retain gestures that evidence emotion—for example, the mother draws her fingers across her neck as she speaks of her relationship with her father.

6. The scene ends with the end of the chapter. Adapt Buddy's last comments to incorporate the thought that Buddy must go by home for clothes anyway.

NARRATOR'S CLOSING LINES

Buddy moves in with his grandfather, but their relationship is short-lived. Something dark from the grandfather's past intrudes upon all their lives, and Buddy must again assess what is important in life.

VERY FAR AWAY FROM ANYWHERE ELSE
Ursula K. Le Guin

The following scene from Ursula Le Guin's *Very Far Away from Anywhere Else* is taken from the scene when, early in the story, Owen visits with Natalie on the bus.

SUGGESTED STAGING

The narrator stands at a lectern. Owen and Natalie are seated on chairs.

Owen   Natalie
  X   X

Narrator
  X

NARRATOR'S OPENING LINES

The characters for this scene, taken from Ursula Le Guin's *Very Far Away from Anywhere Else*, are Owen, a high school senior who prefers walking or riding the bus to school instead of driving the new car he didn't want, read by _____, and Natalie, a quiet musician and also a senior, read by _____. I, _____, am the narrator.

It is raining as Owen gets on the bus and his knapsack drips water on Natalie's knee. He moves the knapsack and it soaks his thigh.

SUGGESTIONS FOR SCRIPTING

1. Start with Owen's saying he is sorry and that his severed artery will stop soon.

2. Instruct Natalie's reader to laugh. Then have Owen continue his speech.

3. Be sure to give the reader clues to Owen's body movements as he slumps in his seat and as he registers surprise and pleasure at Natalie's laughter.

4. After Owen asks her why she has no time, ignore the passages about his thoughts. After she laughs, continue with his prescription for two aspirins and a tourniquet.

5. Natalie's voice records her change in mood from laughter to fierceness about music.

6. Do not have Owen get up, but close the scene having Owen say, "This is my stop. So long."

NARRATOR'S CLOSING LINES

A very close friendship develops between Owen and Natalie. Both are talented and have dreams, but at times find love and priorities to be at odds.

THE CATALOGUE OF THE UNIVERSE
Margaret Mahy

This suggested script is taken from chapter 1 where Angela and her mother, Dido, visit on the veranda.

SUGGESTED STAGING

The narrator stands at a lectern; Angela and Dido sit on the floor.

Angela
X
           Dido
X

Narrator
X

NARRATOR'S OPENING LINES

We are reading a scene from Margaret Mahy's *The Catalogue of the Universe*. The characters in this scene are beautiful Angela May, read by _____, and her free-spirited mother, Dido, read by _____. I, _____, am the narrator.

Angela has awakened at two o'clock in the morning. Outside her window she watches Dido scything. Moonlight floods the scene, and city lights twinkle in the distance. When Dido pauses, Angela scrambles out the window and sits on the veranda and Dido joins her.

SUGGESTIONS FOR SCRIPTING

1. Begin the scene with Angela's asking whether Dido is okay.

2. Angela adores her mother, a gentle but independent spirit. Provide directions to help the readers communicate the emotions.

3. Adapt the lines so that both characters may remain seated on the veranda.

4. Include gestures, such as Angela's putting her hand over her heart.

5. Add to Angela's speech about true love the further explanation, "My old friend Tycho and I are listing romantic ideas."

6. End the scene with Angela's telling Dido that she knows best.

NARRATOR'S CLOSING LINES

Dido, sensing the depth of Angela's desire to know about her father, looks inquiringly at her before they hug goodnight. This night, as other times when Angela has asked about her father, Dido's responses are mysterious and evasive. However, Angela is determined to know her father, and she eventually introduces herself to him in his office. The result is a confrontation that shatters the gentle and romantic fantasy that Dido has created throughout her childhood and that leads her to a new relationship with Tycho.

LISA, BRIGHT AND DARK
John Neufeld

A suggested script from John Neufeld's *Lisa, Bright and Dark* begins with the first lines of chapter 1.

SUGGESTED STAGING
The narrator stands at a lectern. Mother, Father, Lisa, and Mary Nell are all seated in straight chairs.

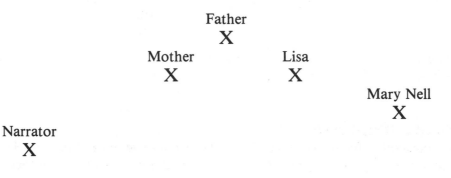

NARRATOR'S OPENING LINES
We will read a portion of the first chapter of *Lisa, Bright and Dark* by John Neufeld. The characters in this scene are Lisa Shilling, a sixteen-year-old, who is afraid she's losing her mind, read by _____; Mary Nell, Lisa's close friend who recognizes Lisa's confusion, read by _____; Lisa's father, a very busy man whose main goal is making money, read by _____; and Lisa's mother, who loves expensive clothes and pays no attention to Lisa or her sister, read by _____. I, _____, am the narrator.

In this scene, Lisa and her friend are finishing dinner at Lisa's house with Lisa's mother and father. Lisa breaks the silence with disturbing news.

SUGGESTIONS FOR SCRIPTING
1. The contrast in emotions should be very apparent. Lisa is distraught, the parents are unconcerned, and Mary Nell is worried. Give the reader clues to Lisa's state with directions like shouting, begging, etc., in parentheses.

2. Close the scene having Lisa's father walk away. Lisa, beginning to quiver, excuses herself and runs to her room. Mary Nell slowly follows Lisa and leaves the mother alone on stage looking helpless and bored as the narrator closes the scene.

NARRATOR'S CLOSING LINES
Mary Nell is discouraged. She has watched Lisa be bright and natural one day, then withdrawn on other days. This scene with the parents makes Mary Nell realize that any effort to help Lisa must come from her friends. Yet, what can they do?

THE OTHER SIDE OF DARK

Joan Lowery Nixon

The following scene from Joan Lowery Nixon's *The Other Side of Dark* begins in chapter 3 as the reporter from the newspaper barges in to interview Stacy.

SUGGESTED STAGING
The narrator stands at a lectern. Stacy and Donna sit in armchairs that do not match. The reporter stands at first and then sits after her second speech.

NARRATOR'S OPENING LINES
We will read a scene from *The Other Side of Dark* by Joan Lowery Nixon. The characters are seventeen-year-old Stacy, who has just awakened from a four-year coma, read by _____; her married sister Donna, read by _____; and a newspaper reporter who has barged in unannounced, read by _____. I, _____, am the narrator.

Four years ago Stacy and her mother were shot. Her mother died, but Stacy went into a rare kind of coma. A reaction to antibiotics finally awakens her, a seventeen-year-old who feels like she's thirteen.

SUGGESTIONS FOR SCRIPTING
1. Have Stacy seated in an arm chair, Donna near her, and the reporter standing until she says her second speech. Then she sits in a chair.

2. Begin the scene with the reporter's asking if anyone told them she was coming.

3. When needed in the script, let Donna pretend to use the phone as though it were on a small table beside her chair.

4. When Stacy asks Brandi, the reporter, if she'd like to comb her hair, let Brandi remain seated and merely answer that it's supposed to look that way.

5. There is a great contrast in the personalities of the pushy Brandi, the protective Donna, and the bewildered Stacy. Be sure to give the readers of the script directions for appropriate voice and body language.

6. Let Donna's soothing voice rather than movement calm Stacy as she talks about the murder. Brandi's voice is contributing to Stacy's emotion.

7. Close the scene as Donna tells Brandi to go away and Brandi merely smiles and thanks them for the interview.

NARRATOR'S CLOSING LINES
Brandi's newspaper story causes Stacy to receive threatening phone calls from her mother's killer. Now, in addition to trying to adjust to changed life and friends, she must cope with fear and the strain of trying to put a face to that shadowy memory.

THE STALKER
Joan Lowery Nixon

The following suggested scene, taken from Joan Lowery Nixon's *The Stalker*, begins in chapter 1 when Jennifer meets the detectives.

SUGGESTED STAGING

The narrator stands at a lectern. The two detectives sit in armchairs. Jennifer and Grannie sit on chairs.

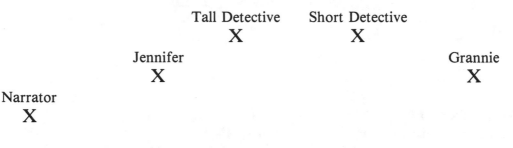

NARRATOR'S OPENING LINES

We will share a scene from *The Stalker* by Joan Lowery Nixon. The characters are the tall detective, read by _____; the short detective, read by _____; seventeen-year-old Jennifer, whose girl friend Bobbie is under suspicion of murder, read by _____; and Grannie, with whom Jennifer lives, read by _____. I, _____, am the narrator.

All are seated in Grannie's living room. The short detective asks the first question.

SUGGESTIONS FOR SCRIPTING

1. Begin by having the short detective ask Jennifer if her name is Jennifer Lee Wilcox.

2. Use the questions that are asked. Do not feel it necessary to make up questions when the narration indicates that the questions go on.

3. Body language is very meaningful in this scene. Be sure to give directions in parentheses to the reader.

4. Close with the end of chapter 1 as Jennifer, gripping the chair and denying that she knows where Bobbie is, stares at the detective.

NARRATOR'S CLOSING LINES

Jennifer knows Bobbie is innocent, and, with the help of a retired detective, she faces danger in order to clear her friend.

Z FOR ZACHARIAH

Robert C. O'Brien

This suggested script is taken from chapter 6 when, on May 29, Mr. Loomis seems to feel better.

SUGGESTED STAGING

The narrator stands at a lectern. Ann and Mr. Loomis sit on chairs.

Ann   Mr. Loomis

X   X

Narrator

X

NARRATOR'S OPENING LINES

We shall share a scene from *Z for Zachariah* by Robert C. O'Brien. The characters are Ann Burden, a resourceful fifteen-year-old, read by _____, and Mr. Loomis, a chemist who wanders into her valley, read by _____. I, _____, am the narrator.

After a nuclear attack Ann survives alone in Burden Valley, thinking she is the last living person on earth. Then Mr. Loomis arrives wearing a safe suit, but he swims in Burden Creek and becomes ill with radiation poisoning. Ann attempts to nurse him back to health. Today, he is sitting in the doorway of the tent as she brings him breakfast.

SUGGESTIONS FOR SCRIPTING

1. Begin the scene as Ann tells Mr. Loomis he is better.

2. Direct the reader for Mr. Loomis to appear suspicious as he questions Ann.

3. After Ann tells him to eat, let Mr. Loomis say, "By the way, my name is John Loomis." Ann will respond with, "And I am Ann Burden."

4. Write a short speech having Ann tell him how the storekeepers and her family drove away and did not return.

5. Create a speech for Mr. Loomis telling about his trip from Ithaca to the valley. Ann's diary description will adapt easily.

6. To end the scene, have Ann tell him she can care for him better in the house.

NARRATOR'S CLOSING LINES

Ann has both hopes and fears as she nurses Mr. Loomis back to health. Things he says in his delirium trouble her. What will the future hold for them?

A FORMAL FEELING

Zibby Oneal

The following suggested scene from *A Formal Feeling* by Zibby Oneal is from chapter 2 when Anne and Spencer are talking soon after she arrives home for vacation.

SUGGESTED STAGING

The narrator stands at a lectern. Anne and Spencer sit on chairs.

Anne   Spencer

X   X

Narrator

X

NARRATOR'S OPENING LINES

We shall share a scene from *A Formal Feeling* by Zibby Oneal. The characters are sixteen-year-old Anne, who has just arrived home from boarding school for winter vacation, read by _____, and Spencer, her genial brother, read by _____. I, _____, am the narrator.

Anne feels uncomfortable about coming home. Her mother has been dead only a year and she resents the new stepmother. She discusses her feelings with her brother who had just brought her home from the airport.

SUGGESTIONS FOR SCRIPTING

1. Begin the scene by having Anne ask Spencer what time the parents come home.

2. Instruct the reader that Anne's voice evidences her resentment of Dory and her inability to forget her mother's death.

3. To end the scene, have Anne remind Spencer he was not *here* last summer.

NARRATOR'S CLOSING LINES

Anne continues to be haunted by her mother's death, and only after she pieces together many memories of earlier days can she reconcile her feelings.

JACOB HAVE I LOVED

Katherine Paterson

The following scene from Katherine Paterson's *Jacob Have I Loved* is taken from the beginning of chapter 4 as Louise and Grandma are awaiting Mother and Caroline's return.

SUGGESTED STAGING

The narrator stands at a lectern. Louise is seated on a chair. Grandma is seated in a rocker.

Louise   Grandma

X   X

Narrator

X

NARRATOR'S OPENING LINES

The characters for this scene, from Katherine Paterson's *Jacob Have I Loved*, are Louise, a twin who feels her sister Caroline gets all the attention and love, read by _____; and Grandma, a crusty old lady who constantly quotes Bible verses, sympathizes with Caroline, and reproves Louise, read by _____. I, _____, am the narrator.

The setting is the Chesapeake Bay area in 1941 just after Pearl Harbor. Louise, now a strong young woman, helps her father with crabbing and tonging for oysters, while Caroline, who is beautiful, talented, and frail, practices her music. Today, Caroline's mother has taken her by ferry to the doctor. Louise is trying to read, and Grandma is rocking with her eyes closed.

SUGGESTIONS FOR SCRIPTING

1. Begin with Grandma's bitter remark that she hates the water.

2. Be sure to have Louise's reader communicate exaggerated patience when she must put down her book.

3. After Louise offers to get coffee for Grandma, let the narrator say: Louise gets coffee, and after Grandma tastes it, she complains that it lacks sugar. Louise has the sugar bowl hidden behind her and feels so happy to have outsmarted Grandma that she begins to whistle "Praise the Lord and Pass the Ammunition."

4. Be sure to note Grandma's sarcasm as she gives her whistling women speech. Her sarcasm changes to shock; then she is so angry she screams.

5. Louise's reader can exaggerate humbleness in contrast to Grandma.

6. After Grandma insists that Louise help her poor mother, let the narrator say: It is useless to argue with Grandma, so Louise gets her jacket and starts to leave. Grandma surprisingly interrupts her exit.

7. Louise remains seated during the narrator's speech and the remainder of the scene. Her voice emphasizes her quiet anger.

8. The scene ends with Grandma's telling her to hurry as she doesn't like waiting alone.

NARRATOR'S CLOSING LINES

Louise's bitterness intensifies as her parents continue to give Caroline their attention and seem to ignore Louise's need to feel she is worth something. Leaving the island becomes a necessity in order for Louise to find her identity and resolve her bitterness.

HATCHET
Gary Paulsen

The suggested scene from *Hatchet* by Gary Paulsen is taken from chapter 1 when Brian is flying to visit his father.

SUGGESTED STAGING

The narrator stands at a lectern. Brian and the pilot sit on chairs.

Brian   Pilot
X   X

Narrator
X

NARRATOR'S OPENING LINES

We shall share a scene from *Hatchet* by Gary Paulsen. The characters are thirteen-year-old Brian, troubled by his parents' divorce, read by _____; and the quiet pilot, intent on his job, read by _____. I, _____, am the narrator.

Brian and the pilot are flying over the Canadian wilderness in a single-engine bush plane. They are on their way to meet Brian's father, whom Brian has not seen since the divorce that shattered his life.

SUGGESTIONS FOR SCRIPTING

1. Begin the scene with the pilot's asking Brian whether he has ever flown in the copilot's seat before.

2. After the pilot takes the controls back, rubs his shoulder, and comments on his aches and pains, have Brian thank him. Then the narrator may say: The pilot is quiet for awhile, but suddenly he grimaces in pain.

3. The pilot is obviously in great pain, as he holds his stomach and says he thinks the pain was caused by something he ate. Brian's reader should reflect his fear as the pilot attempts to call for help, then screams that his chest is coming apart.

4. Omit the pages of description and continue with Brian's asking, obviously into a mike, if anybody is listening.

5. Close the scene with his screaming for somebody to help him.

NARRATOR'S CLOSING LINES

The plane crashes and Brian must spend fifty-four days in the wilderness with his only survival tool being the hatchet his mother gave him. During his experience he also discovers how to survive his parents' divorce.

FATHER FIGURE
Richard Peck

The following scene from *Father Figure* by Richard Peck is taken from chapter 2 when Byron and Jim are at the funeral home the night before their mother's funeral.

SUGGESTED STAGING
The narrator stands at a lectern. Winifred, Jim, and Byron are seated on chairs.

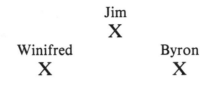

Jim
X

Winifred
X

Byron
X

Narrator
X

NARRATOR'S OPENING LINES
We will share a scene from Richard Peck's *Father Figure*. The characters are seventeen-year-old Jim Atwater, read by _____; his younger brother Byron, read by _____; and Winifred High-smith, an old friend of their mother, read by _____. I, _____, am the narrator.

The boys are sitting in the funeral home the night before the funeral of their mother, an ill woman who has committed suicide. Winifred Highsmith, whom they do not know, comes over, sits down, and introduces herself.

SUGGESTIONS FOR SCRIPTING
1. As the scene opens, have the three characters seated as Winifred asks whether Jim is Jim Atwater.

2. Be sure to note for the reader the change in Winifred's tone as she feels critical, sympathetic, and angry.

3. Jim is nervous, defensive, and bewildered. Give the reader directions for interpreting his emotional state.

4. End the scene with Winifred's getting ready to leave and telling the boys that they will be fine.

NARRATOR'S CLOSING LINES
The two brothers survive the funeral, but after eight years, how can Jim turn over his role of being a father figure for Byron? Is it fair that a father he doesn't know expects him to do so?

REMEMBERING THE GOOD TIMES
Richard Peck

The following scene from Richard Peck's *Remembering the Good Times* begins in chapter 6 as Buck meets Kate in the orchard after having spent the summer in Cleveland with his mother.

SUGGESTED STAGING

The narrator stands at a lectern; Buck and Kate sit on the floor.

	Buck	Kate
	X	X
Narrator		
X		

NARRATOR'S OPENING LINES

We will read a scene from *Remembering the Good Times* by Richard Peck. The characters are Buck, who lives with his dad in a trailer house, read by _____; and Kate, who lives with her eccentric grandmother Polly, read by _____. I, _____, am the narrator.

Buck and his friend Trav, whose parents are wealthy, were often in Kate's kitchen playing board games with Polly making the foursome. As Buck returns from a summer in Cleveland with his mother, he feels jealous that Trav has been with Kate all summer while he was away. On his return, he finds Kate alone in the orchard reading.

SUGGESTIONS FOR SCRIPTING

1. Begin with Kate's statement that Polly is right and Kate should never marry either Buck or Trav.

2. Be sure to give the readers of the script directions to show the change in Kate's mood from happiness at seeing Buck to concern for Trav's mental health and anger at Buck's lack of concern.

3. To end the scene, have Buck jealously ask Kate what Trav talks to her about.

NARRATOR'S CLOSING LINES

Kate's concerns about Trav are justified. Change comes to the orchard, tragedy strikes, and only wise Polly can help the community accept responsibility and Buck and Kate face reality.

WHAT HAPPENED IN HAMELIN

Gloria Skurzynski

The following suggested scene from *What Happened in Hamelin* by Gloria Skurzynski is taken from chapter 2 when Geist meets the stranger Gast under the bridge.

SUGGESTED STAGING

The narrator stands at a lectern. Geist and Gast sit on the floor.

Gast   Geist
X   X

Narrator
X

NARRATOR'S OPENING LINES

The scene we shall share is from *What Happened in Hamelin* by Gloria Skurzynski. The characters are Geist, a fourteen-year-old orphan, read by _____; and Gast, a flute-playing stranger who seems to know how to rid the town of rats, read by _____. I, _____, am the narrator.

The stranger Gast drowns a rat and then drops it so Master Hermann, a member of the town council, thinks it died in his shop. When Master Hermann asks Gast if he will rid them of rats, Gast says he'll think about it. He will tell Geist the solution to the town's problem if Geist will meet him under the bridge after the church bell rings vespers. As the scene opens, Geist has just gone to the bridge.

SUGGESTIONS FOR SCRIPTING

1. Begin the scene by having Geist ask Gast if the dead rat was placed there by him.

2. End the scene by having Gast say that Geist is to tell Master Hermann that Gast requests the meeting.

NARRATOR'S CLOSING LINES

The stranger first appears in Hamelin in 1284; and before he leaves, Geist is involved in a sinister scheme that ends in tragedy.

SINGULARITY
William Sleator

This suggested script is taken from Chapter 6 where Barry, after being locked in the playhouse, demands an explanation from his twin brother Harry.

SUGGESTED STAGING

The narrator stands at a lectern; Harry and Barry sit on stools. Lucy also sits on a stool.

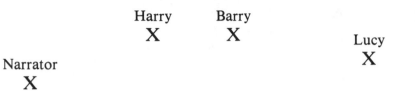

NARRATOR'S OPENING LINES

The script that we are reading is from William Sleator's *Singularity*, a science fiction novel. The characters are a pair of sixteen-year-old twin brothers and their neighbor Lucy. Harry, the patient and accommodating brother, is read by _____; Barry, the brother who resents having a twin, is read by _____; and Lucy is read by _____. I, _____, am the narrator.

Barry and Harry have traveled from their home in Boston to a farm in Illinois so that they can watch over the farmhouse their mother has recently inherited. Mystery surrounds the farm and especially a metal building that is known as the "playhouse." Near the playhouse are animal skeletons, and there have been strange stories told about the disappearance and the rapid aging of animals who have strayed near the site. On the morning that Barry and Harry begin their exploration of the playhouse, the door slams shut behind Harry, leaving Barry momentarily alone in the building. Harry unlocks the door, steps back inside, and finds that Barry is lying asleep on the cot. The room has been cleaned, and there is stubble on the lower half of Barry's face.

SUGGESTIONS FOR SCRIPTING

1. Write Harry's first lines communicating his demand that Barry stop.

2. Barry is furious; Harry is bewildered and frightened. Provide instructions for the readers so that the emotions of the two characters are clearly communicated to the audience.

3. Clarify that Barry has eaten survival biscuits by having Harry ask, "Why is this box of survival biscuits half empty? Why are all those wrappers scattered on the floor?"

4. Provide instructions for nonverbal communication to be directed to the audience through the body language of the readers. For example, instruct the reader for Barry to roll his eyes and groan when the text describes those actions.

5. Include the following narrator's lines which describe the pair's movement from the playhouse back to the farmhouse: The two walk back to the farmhouse to use the telephone in the kitchen.

6. Omit Lucy's invitation that the brothers join her for a swim.

7. End the scene with Harry's observation that time goes faster in the playhouse.

NARRATOR'S CLOSING LINES

Their efforts to explain that rapid passage of time lead the three to a dangerous passageway to another universe, and the unearthly force they discover changes the relationship between the twin brothers forever.

THE GIFT OF SARAH BARKER

Jane Yolen

The following suggested scene from *The Gift of Sarah Barker* by Jane Yolen is taken from chapter 11 when Sarah meets Abel in the barn.

SUGGESTED STAGING

The narrator stands at a lectern. Sarah and Abel sit on stools.

Sarah   Abel

X   X

Narrator

X

NARRATOR'S OPENING LINES

We would like to read a scene from *The Gift of Sarah Barker* by Jane Yolen. The characters are Sarah Barker, a sensitive teenager, read by _____, and Abel Church, a young man who is attracted to Sarah, read by _____. I, _____, am the narrator.

The setting is a Shaker community in Massachusetts in 1854. Here men and women work together but live separated. Marriage is not allowed. It is wrong for a boy to even touch a girl. Sarah and Abel meet by accident and cannot forget each other. Abel asks Sarah to meet him because he needs someone to talk to. On this night they walk to the barn to talk.

SUGGESTIONS FOR SCRIPTING

1. Begin the scene with Abel's comment that he is afraid she will be offended by the smell of cows.

2. When Sarah begins to cry, do not have Abel move toward her. Let his gentle voice soothe her as he tells her it is all right because he is there.

3. Omit Sarah's stumbling and Abel's asking if she is hurt. Ignore the "no" in her following speech and start the speech with her remembering something more.

4. End the scene with Abel's saying he does not know either, but he wants them to discover friendship together.

NARRATOR'S CLOSING LINES

Sarah and Abel know they will be required to leave the Shaker community if they are caught talking to each other. Yet, how can they give up their newfound friendship?

THE PIGMAN
Paul Zindel

The following scene from Paul Zindel's *The Pigman* is taken from chapter 5 when John and Lorraine go to Mr. Pignati's house to collect the money.

SUGGESTED STAGING

The narrator stands at a lectern. John and Lorraine are seated in straight chairs; Mr. Pignati is seated in an armchair.

John   Lorraine

X   X   Mr. Pignati

X

Narrator

X

NARRATOR'S OPENING LINES

We shall share a scene from *The Pigman* by Paul Zindel. The characters are Lorraine and John, two high school sophomore friends who feel lonely and neglected by their parents, read by _____ and _____; and Mr. Pignati, a lonely old man, read by _____. I, _____, am the narrator.

Lorraine and John have telephoned Mr. Pignati to trick him into giving them ten dollars for a supposed charity. They are embarrassed at their deception, but John needs money so they go to Mr. Pignati's house to collect the money. They have picked his number at random from the phone book, so they have never met him. He ushers them into the living room and asks them to sit down. He seems very happy to see them.

SUGGESTIONS FOR SCRIPTING

1. Begin by having Mr. Pignati say he just got back from the zoo.

2. Be sure to give John's and Lorraine's readers clues to their changing moods—laughter, nervousness, kindness, impatience, and embarrassment.

3. Mr. Pignati's moods change from happiness at their arrival to excitement in the game and depression as they prepare to leave.

4. End the scene when Lorraine hesitantly says they have not seen his pigs.

NARRATOR'S CLOSING LINES

Mr. Pignati shows them a room full of glass, clay, and marble pigs of all sizes and colors. He tells them he began his wife's pig collection before they were married to remind her of him because his name is Pignati. Lorraine and John leave, and the next day they go to the zoo with Mr. Pignati. A strange friendship develops with this lonely old man who is trying to forget his wife's death. Although it ends in tragedy, Mr. Pignati gives them a new realization about life.

ANNOTATED BIBLIOGRAPHY

BIBLIOGRAPHY
FOR COMPLETED SCRIPTS

Brontë, Emily. *Wuthering Heights*. New York: Dutton, 1907.
    Mr. Lockwood unravels the history of Catherine's rejection of Heathcliff and the effects of his revenge.

Cervantes, Miguel de. *The Ingenious Gentleman Don Quixote de la Mancha*. Translated by John Ormsby. New York: Dodd, 1893.
    The Spanish knight-errant Don Quixote, determined to right every wrong, dresses in full armor and, on horseback, roams the world.

Crane, Stephen. *The Red Badge of Courage*. New York: Appleton-Century-Crofts, 1895.
    Henry Fleming, a soldier, experiences realistic but diverse emotions as he enlists, awaits battle, fights, flees, and fights again.

Dickens, Charles. *The Personal History of David Copperfield*. New York: Hurst, 1884.
    The history of David Copperfield, Dickens's largely autobiographical account, traces David's life from birth through adulthood in nineteenth-century England.

_____. *A Tale of Two Cities*. New York: Crowell, 1904.
    Imprisonment, betrayal, the threat of the guillotine, and sacrifice characterize the life and times of the Manettes who live in France and England during the French Revolution.

Eliot, George [pseud.]. *Silas Marner*. New York: Harper, 1903.
    Silas Marner, a miserly weaver who has lived alone for years following a false accusation of theft, ends his despair when he becomes the guardian of a small child.

Hawthorne, Nathaniel. *The House of the Seven Gables*. In *The Complete Writings of Nathaniel Hawthorne*. Vol. 7. Boston: Houghton Mifflin, 1903.
    Living in poverty in the house of seven gables, Hepzibah Pyncheon, her brother Clifford, and her cousin Phoebe are, with Judge Pyncheon's sudden death, freed from his threats and become his wealthy inheritors.

_____. *The Scarlet Letter*. In *The Complete Writings of Nathaniel Hawthorne*. Vol. 6. Boston: Houghton Mifflin, 1903.
    The sin of adultery in eighteenth-century Boston affects the lives of four characters: Hester, who is sentenced to wear a scarlet letter; Pearl, her child; Arthur Dimmesdale, her unconfessed partner; and Roger Chillingworth, her revenge-seeking husband.

Irving, Washington. *Rip Van Winkle*. New York: Doubleday and McClure, 1897.

Rip, having been asleep for twenty years, awakens to an unfamiliar world, but happily one that includes neither a nagging wife nor the expectation that the old gentleman should be gainfully employed.

London, Jack. *White Fang*. New York: Macmillan, 1906.

White Fang, part dog and part wolf, learns that survival of the fittest always requires strength and intelligence and often the ability to adapt to an abusive master as well as a patient one.

Poe, Edgar Allan. "The Purloined Letter." In *The Complete Works of Edgar Allan Poe*. Vol 3. Akron, Ohio: Werner, 1908.

The prefect of the Paris police is baffled in the attempt to recover a stolen letter and seeks the advice of Dupin, a noted detective, who finds the letter by looking not in an obscure place, but rather in an obvious place.

Shelley, Mary Wollstonecraft. *Frankenstein*. Philadelphia: Lippincott, 1897.

Victor Frankenstein assembles a living monster who, as an outcast from society, turns upon humankind and especially upon his creator.

Stevenson, Robert Louis. *The Strange Case of Dr. Jekyll and Mr. Hyde*. New York: Scribner's, 1895.

The respectable Dr. Jekyll, who leads a dual life by becoming the callous and wicked Mr. Hyde at night, is overtaken and destroyed by the evil side of his personality.

Twain, Mark [pseud.]. *A Connecticut Yankee in King Arthur's Court*. In *The Writings of Mark Twain*. Vol. 16. New York: Harper, 1899.

A Yankee is knocked unconscious and awakens to find himself in sixth-century England, thus providing an avenue through which Twain satirizes not only Camelot, but also his own society.

_____. *The Adventures of Tom Sawyer*. In *The Writings of Mark Twain*. Vol. 12. New York: Harper, 1903.

Playing pranks and sharing adventures with Huck Finn, Tom Sawyer becomes the hero of every boy in town.

Wilde, Oscar. *The Picture of Dorian Gray*. New York: Charterhouse, 1904.

Dorian Gray, who sells his soul for eternal youth, hides the portrait that records both his aging and the outward signs of his evil life until, in an attempt to destroy it, he destroys himself.

BIBLIOGRAPHY
FOR SUGGESTED SCRIPTS

Avi. *Wolf Rider: A Tale of Terror*. New York: Bradbury, 1986.

Fifteen-year-old Andy receives a phone call from a man claiming he has killed Nina; and, in his efforts to make others believe him, he estranges himself from his father and faces personal danger.

Bess, Clayton. *Tracks*. Boston: Houghton Mifflin, 1986.

Seventeen-year-old Monroe and his eleven-year-old brother Blue discover many kinds of people as they ride the rails during the Great Depression.

Bickham, Jack. *All the Days Were Summer*. Garden City, New York: Doubleday, 1981.
Twelve-year-old Danny Davidson and Rudi, a German POW, build a friendship as Danny seeks his advice about the training of a blind German shepherd puppy.

Blume, Judy. *Tiger Eyes*. New York: Bradbury, 1981.
Fifteen-year-old Davey Wexler cannot cope with her father's murder, until a young man who also faces tragedy helps her to adjust.

Bradbury, Ray. *Something Wicked This Way Comes*. New York: Knopf, 1983.
Cooger and Dark's Pandemonium Shadow Show arrives in Green Town and mysteriously lures the people with promises to satisfy their secret dreams, but Will Halloway and his middle-aged father understand the price and defeat the dark force.

Brooks, Bruce. *The Moves Make the Man*. New York: Harper & Row, 1984.
When thirteen-year-old Jayfox, the only black student in his junior high school, attempts to befriend an emotionally troubled classmate, he takes on problems for which there are no immediate solutions.

Butterworth, W. E. *LeRoy and the Old Man*. New York: Four Winds, 1980.
Running away from a Chicago neighborhood gang that seeks to prevent his identifying them to the police, LeRoy travels to the home of his paternal grandfather, a fisherman in Christian, Mississippi, where he learns the values of the demanding and resourceful old man.

Clapp, Patricia. *The Tamarack Tree*. New York: Lothrop, Lee and Shepard, 1986.
Rosemary Leigh, a British girl, faces questions and hardships as she lives through the seige of Vicksburg during the Civil War.

Colman, Hila. *Weekend Sisters*. New York: William Morrow, 1985.
Fourteen-year-old Amanda must share her father with a selfish, deceitful stepsister when he remarries, and she fears she is losing her father's love.

Conrad, Pam. *Prairie Songs*. New York: Harper & Row, 1985.
The arrival of Dr. Berryman and his frail, helpless wife changes the life of the Downings, a close, brave pioneer family in Nebraska.

Cormier, Robert. *I Am the Cheese*. New York: Pantheon, 1977.
Adam Farmer must cope with the interrogations of ruthless government officials who are conspirators in his parents' murders.

Dixon, Paige. *May I Cross Your Golden River?* New York: Atheneum, 1975.
Jordan Phillips, an eighteen-year-old who has Lou Gehrig's disease, survives only a few months; however, he finds and gives courage and hope in his warm, close family and the values they share.

Duncan, Lois. *I Know What You Did Last Summer*. Boston: Little, Brown, 1973.
Four friends, trying to hide a hit-and-run accident, are sought by an attacker seeking revenge.

Dygard, Thomas J. *Wilderness Peril*. New York: William Morrow, 1983.
    Two high school graduates taking a Minnesota wilderness canoe trip must cope with a desperate hijacker with $750,000.

Garfield, Leon. *Footsteps*. New York: Delacorte, 1980.
    His father's confession before his death causes William to face many dangers as he tries to make amends.

Geller, Mark. *My Life in the Seventh Grade*. New York: Harper & Row, 1986.
    Marvin Berman records in his diary the problems he encounters in seventh grade and the friendships he makes.

Golding, William. *Lord of the Flies*. New York: Coward, McCann, & Geoghegan, 1962.
    A group of English schoolboys who are stranded on a coral island experience an unrelenting descent into anarchy and savagery.

Greene, Betty. *Summer of My German Soldier*. New York: Dial, 1973.
    Patty Bergen needs friendship and love; and she finds it with Anton Reiker, a POW in World War II.

Guest, Judith. *Ordinary People*. New York: Viking, 1976.
    Conrad, following his brother's death and his own attempt at suicide and subsequent stay in a mental hospital, is sent home to cope with loving parents who make mistakes, a re-entry into school and his circle of friends, and the final resolution of his ambivalent feelings.

Guy, Rosa. *The Disappearance*. New York: Delacorte, 1979.
    After being taken into the Aimsley household, Imamu Jones is accused in the disappearance of young Perk Aimsley, and he must overcome his feelings of fear and betrayal in order to solve the mystery and prove his innocence.

Hall, Lynn. *The Solitary*. New York: Scribner's, 1986.
    After living with an aunt and uncle who do not want her, seventeen-year-old Jane moves back to the dilapidated Arkansas house where her mother killed her father years earlier.

Hinton, S. E. *Tex*. New York: Delacorte, 1979.
    Fifteen-year-old Tex and his older brother Mason (Mace) must face the reality of poverty and growing up as they survive without the help of their rodeo-riding father.

Hunter, Mollie. *Cat, Herself*. New York: Harper & Row, 1986.
    Although Cat McPhie's father taught her the skills of Scottish traveller men, she has difficulty altering the restricting role placed on the traveller women.

Irwin, Hadley. *Abby, My Love*. New York: Atheneum, 1985.
    Chip and Abby's high school friendship is marred by the changing moods of Abby caused by her father's sexual abuse of her, but with help Abby is able to control her life.

Kerr, M. E. *Gentlehands*. New York: Harper & Row, 1978.
    Buddy Boyle gets acquainted with his rich estranged grandfather as he tries to impress a wealthy summer girl, but a heartbreaking revelation spoils their relationship.

Le Guin, Ursula K. *Very Far Away from Anywhere Else*. New York: Atheneum, 1976.
    Owen and Natalie are talented high school seniors who find their dreams of the future not always compatible with a friendship that turns to love.

Mahy, Margaret. *The Catalogue of the Universe*. New York: Atheneum, 1986.
    Angela May's childhood fantasy, created by her mother Dido, is destroyed when she finds and confronts her unknown father; however, she discovers a new and romantic relationship with her old friend Tycho.

Neufeld, John. *Lisa, Bright and Dark*. New York: S. G. Phillips, 1969.
    Lisa knows she is losing her mind, but only her three friends will try to help her.

Nixon, Joan Lowery. *The Other Side of Dark*. New York: Delacorte, 1986.
    Seventeen-year-old Stacy awakens from a four-year coma caused by a gunshot wound. She must try to remember the face of the man who shot her and killed her mother and identify him before he kills her.

_____. *The Stalker*. New York: Delacorte, 1985.
    Seventeen-year-old Jennifer and a retired detective try to prove the innocence of Jennifer's best friend who is accused of murder.

O'Brien, Robert C. *Z for Zachariah*. New York: Atheneum, 1974.
    After a nuclear war, Ann Burden survives for a year believing she is the last person on earth, only to be threatened by a man she befriends.

Oneal, Zibby. *A Formal Feeling*. New York: Viking, 1982.
    Sixteen-year-old Anne resents her stepmother until time and memories help her accept the pain of her mother's death.

Paterson, Katherine. *Jacob Have I Loved*. New York: Harper & Row, 1980.
    Because Louise feels unworthy as her parents give all their attention to twin sister Caroline, she must finally leave home to resolve her bitterness.

Paulsen, Gary. *Hatchet*. New York: Bradbury, 1987.
    Thirteen-year-old Brian survives for fifty-four days alone in the Canadian woods after an airplane crash.

Peck, Richard. *Father Figure*. New York: Viking, 1978.
    After being his brother's substitute father for eight years, Jim resents the father's attempt to assume the role.

_____. *Remembering the Good Times*. New York: Delacorte, 1985.
    Buck, Kate, and Trav are high school friends, but friendship is not enough to keep adult pressures from contributing to a tragedy.

Skurzynski, Gloria. *What Happened in Hamelin*. New York: Four Winds, 1979.
    A fourteen-year-old orphan tells the sinister tale of his involvement in the tragic Pied Piper story.

Sleator, William. *Singularity*. New York: Dutton, 1985.
    Two sixteen-year-old twins discover a fantastic force capable of speeding up time, and one allows that force to change their relationship forever.

Yolen, Jane. *The Gift of Sarah Barker*. New York: Viking, 1981.
    Two teenagers in a Shaker village must decide whether that way of life is right for them.

Zindel, Paul. *The Pigman*. New York: Harper & Row, 1968.
    Two high school sophomores make friends with a lonely old man who, in tragedy, changes their outlook on life.

INDEX